The
Secrets of
Telephone
Selling

How to Make Calls that Sell!

Neil Johnson

KOGAN
PAGE

To Anne, without whom life would be meaningless

First published in 1994

Apart from any fair dealing for the purposes of research or private study, or criticism or review, as permitted under the Copyright, Designs and Patents Act, 1988, this publication may only be reproduced, stored or transmitted, in any form or by any means, with the prior permission in writing of the publishers, or in the case of reprographic reproduction in accordance with the terms of licences issued by the Copyright Licensing Agency. Enquiries concerning reproduction outside those terms should be sent to the publishers at the undermentioned address:

Kogan Page Limited
120 Pentonville Road
London N1 9JN

© Neil Johnson 1994

British Library Cataloguing in Publication Data

A CIP record for this book is available from the British Library.

ISBN 0–7494–1219–4

Typeset by DP Photosetting, Aylesbury, Bucks
Printed and bound in Great Britain by
Clays Ltd., St Ives plc

Contents

Introduction

Why you should read this book

Human ingenuity is at work in every corner of the globe.

As you read these words, there are machines that are carefully feeling their way towards Jupiter and beyond; machines that are inching their way across ocean floors and machines that are rhythmically pumping blood inside human bodies.

There are installations turning water into electricity, plant matter into ships, and an obscure element called silicon into the most voracious calculating machines the world has ever known.

There are instruments analysing the temperature on Mars, the wind speed in the Atlantic and the eating habits of animals who roamed the earth millions of years ago.

There are laboratories producing life-saving drugs, new and better forms of vegetable, and thousands upon thousands of new products to enhance and improve human life into the twenty-first century.

And yet, despite all of this, despite this overwhelming evidence of Man's ingenuity and inventiveness in so many different fields, there is one type of product that has so far eluded him: one type of product that has proved impossible for him to produce: the product that sells itself.

That is why you should read this book!

What sort of person do you have to be in order to sell?

There is a popular myth that only someone who is a complete extrovert can become a salesperson. This is nonsense! Almost anyone can sell and almost anyone who works hard can sell well.

It makes no difference whether you are male or female, old or young, extrovert or introvert, or whether you are ambitious or unambitious, educated or uneducated. You can still be a success in sales.

What's more, there are no sales qualifications as such: no degrees, diplomas or courses that you can take in order to quality as a salesperson. Nearly all sales training (such as it is) is conducted by companies, who train their own staff to sell company products. In many cases this in-house training is so skimpy that most salespeople end up learning on the job.

OK, you may ask, if there are no particular personal characteristics or formal qualifications required, what do I need in order to be able to sell? After all, selling is bound to be easier for some people than for others.

I can think of only two things to say in answer to this. First, if you honestly do not enjoy talking to people, then selling is not for you. Second, if you do enjoy talking to people and have a willingness to learn how to talk on the telephone and a readiness to practise what you learn, then you'll do fine.

Don't take my word for it, however. Read the book and then make up your own mind!

Author's note

In order to make this book as simple and as readable as possible, I have chosen to avoid writing 'he/she', 'him/her', 'his/her' whenever gender is mentioned. Instead, I attribute a single gender to all my characters which allows the text to flow without interruption. I emphasise that this is done purely for stylistic reasons. Thus the words 'he', 'him' and 'his' are at all times interchangeable with the words 'she', 'her' and 'hers' and vice versa.

Part One
What You Must Know Before You Start Selling

1. Telephone Selling Explained

Tele-sales: the world's fastest-growing method of selling

There are thousands of different products and services sold over the phone every hour of every day: everything from Siberian oil to New Zealand lamb, from Jumbo jets to diamonds and from airtime on television to plots in the cemetery.

Selling by phone is the fastest-growing sales technique in the world. It's fast, it's cheap and it fits in perfectly with satellite communications, fax machines and all the other gadgetry. Fortunately, despite its fast-moving, hi-tech image, telephone selling still cannot be done by machines: it needs people, salespeople. That is where we come in.

What is telephone selling really all about?

In essence, telephone selling is about talking and listening on the telephone.

Talking to people

Telephone selling is all about talking to people: lots and lots and lots of people. Of course, you don't talk to them about just anything – you talk to them about your product, but the essential thing about it, the thing that makes it different from most other jobs, is the fact that it involves talking to lots and lots and lots of people.

Talking to buyers

So who do you talk to? You talk to buyers: people who buy products for their business or company. You talk to managing directors, marketing directors, production directors, purchasing managers, personnel managers, production managers and sales managers – in short, anyone whose job involves buying the product you are selling.

Talking to buyers about benefits
What exactly do you talk to these buyers about? You talk to them about the benefits of your product, you talk to them about what your product will do for them and how it will help them to achieve their objectives.

Talking to buyers about benefits over time
Reaching agreement with a buyer over the phone takes time. This is because your buyer needs time to recognize the value of your product, time to examine it, time to understand how he can make use of it and time to adjust to the idea of spending his money on it. You will, therefore, need to make not one, but several telephone calls, in order to satisfy his need for time. In other words, telephone selling is really 'talking through' your product with the buyer, over a period of time, rather than trying to dazzle him with one spectacular presentation.

Talking until your buyer agrees to buy
The ultimate point of all this talk is to convince your listener to buy your product. You may not always be successful – indeed, you may only ever convince a tiny minority of your listeners to buy whatever it is you are selling – but you must never forget that your ultimate aim is to persuade people to *buy*!

The role that sales people play in business
No one can properly understand selling unless they understand the role that salespeople play in business.

All companies and commercial enterprises need to buy a wide variety of things for their business.

To begin with, they need to buy office accommodation. After that, they need to recruit staff, so they need to buy advertising space or else buy the services of a recruitment agency. At the same time, they have to buy a range of office products, such as telephones, furniture, computers, photocopiers, stationery, coffee machines and so on. They also need to buy a range of services, such as insurance, cleaning, maintenance, security and transport.

Of course, they will also need to buy a range of specific items for the specific business they are engaged in. For example, if they are manufacturers, they need to buy raw materials; if they are distributors, they need to buy products to distribute; and if they sell a particular service (eg, advertising), they need to buy expertise.

Finally, in order to gain customers for their product, they have to buy advertising or publicity or any number of promotional products and services.

In other words, all companies spend a great deal of time and money buying and replacing a wide range of different products which are essential to their commercial performance.

The specific people who do all this buying will vary from company to company and from purchase to purchase. Usually, expensive or important products are bought only by directors, while cheaper, less important ones are bought by less senior staff. However, all company buyers, whoever they are and whatever they are buying, have one thing in common: they depend upon salespeople for what to buy.

What this means is that, in practice, most buyers depend upon salespeople to talk to them and keep them up to date about what they can buy.

More specifically, buyers depend upon sales people to explain to them the precise benefits of the product in question, and how it can help them to run their business more efficiently.

Without salespeople to ring them up and keep them informed, most buyers would find it very difficult to buy the best products at the best price, and their companies would suffer accordingly.

So always remember, *buyers need sales people to talk to them and explain the products they are selling.*

What benefits are there from learning how to sell over the phone?

You will benefit in a number of ways.

You will acquire three valuable skills

First, by developing the art of talking to people you will greatly enhance your ability to solve problems and get things done.

Second, the telephone is a very powerful instrument if used properly. By improving your telephone technique and learning how to deal with problems over the phone, you will acquire a very practical and highly marketable skill.

Thirdly, telephone selling will sharpen up your ability to explain things clearly and simply and to justify yourself in the process: another very useful skill for anyone.

You will obtain greater job opportunities

To begin with, a great many people fail in jobs and in interviews, not because they lack talent or knowledge but because they cannot communicate that talent or knowledge to other people. Because selling is largely about communication, anyone who has learned how to sell has also learned how to communicate and is, therefore, much more likely to be able to present themselves and their ideas.

In terms of specific job opportunities, tele-sales experience is ideal for any other type of sales job, including sales management, and is very useful for jobs in sales promotion, purchasing, marketing, advertising, public relations, personnel, market research, publishing and most types of management.

It might even enable you to set up your own business. A number of small businesses, for example, require only an office, a telephone and an ability to sell in order to get started.

You can earn good money
Generally, salespeople have higher earnings and higher earning capacity than most other company personnel. Sometimes, this differential can be enormous. In addition, by moving from tele-sales into general sales, a salesperson can gain access to a range of company benefits which are usually reserved for the favoured few. Company cars and entertainment allowances are two such benefits.

What sorts of companies employ tele-sales staff?

All sorts of companies use tele-sales staff: for example, manufacturing companies (those that make their own products), distribution companies (those that simply distribute other people's products) and service companies (those that offer a particular service rather than a product). In short, just about every sort of company has some use for tele-sales staff. In addition, there are several specialist tele-sales companies that do nothing but sell other companies' products and services over the telephone.

What sorts of thing can be sold over the telephone?

In theory, almost anything; but in practice, some products also need to be explained and demonstrated face to face. This is usually where either the product is especially complicated and/or expensive (eg, computers), or where its appearance or fit is important (eg, houses, clothes etc). In other words, the simpler and more standardized the product, the easier it is to sell over the phone.

Do tele-sales staff have to sell face-to-face as well?

Some do, some don't. Generally speaking, it is more common for salespeople to mix telephone selling with a certain amount of face-to-face work. This is because some customers prefer not to buy products they have not seen from sales people they have not met. Face-to-face meetings can also be very important in helping to reassure customers and ironing out any telephone objections which they may have raised to buying the product in question.

What sort of tele-sales training will I be given?

In my experience, companies devote very little time and effort to sales training of any kind, let alone tele-sales training. That is one of the big problems facing anyone who wants to go into sales. It is as if companies expect the people they recruit to have already been trained somewhere else. Of course, there are some notable exceptions, where sales staff receive excellent training, but these are few and far between.

What help will I receive when I start selling on the phone?

Usually you will receive two things. First, an explanation of the product that you will be selling, including how it compares with other products on the market. Second, you will sometimes be given some form of sales script. As the name suggests, this is a sheet of paper or card detailing what to say to customers when you phone them. It is meant to act more as an *aide-mémoire* than a precise instruction as to exactly what to say, but some companies do insist on you sticking fairly closely to the form of words used, at least until you become familiar with what you are selling.

Neither the product explanation that you will receive nor the script that you may be given are in any sense an adequate substitute for proper tele-sales training.

Unless you are lucky enough to join a company that offers proper tele-sales training, you will probably have to do most of your learning the hard way – on your own, by a process of trial and error. Apart from reading this book, the only advice I can give you is to keep your ears open. Nearly all tele-sales offices contain one or two good sales people, from whom you can learn a great deal. Listen to what they have to say over the phone and how they say it. This is how I learned to sell, so I know it works.

2. Introduction to the Three Basic Types of Tele-sales Call

For most salespeople selling most products, there are three basic types of tele-sales call they have to make:

- The canvassing call.
- The presentation call.
- The closing call.

The canvassing call

A salesperson makes this type of call when he is ringing to introduce himself, his product and his company to a new customer.

He has several things to do. First, he must find out the name of the person at the customer company who is responsible for buying the type of product that he (the salesperson) is selling. He must then introduce himself and his product, together with the company he represents.

After that, he must find out more about the customer. For example, the precise nature and extent of the customer's business, and whether and to what extent the customer already uses products similar to those the salesperson has for sale.

Finally, unless the customer has absolutely no need for the product, he will arrange to send the company some information about it and to call back in a few days to discuss the matter further.

In short, we can list the aims of the canvassing call as follows:

- To introduce the salesperson and his company/product to the appropriate buyer.

- To find out more about the customer and to what extent he needs the product being offered.
- To arrange for the customer to receive information and/or samples of the product.
- To arrange for the salesperson to make a follow-up call to discuss the matter further.

Example

Suppose X Ltd moves into a new warehouse and office complex. A local fax machine company hears of this and one of its salespeople telephones X Ltd to introduce himself and the various fax machines supplied by his company. After establishing that X Ltd does not have a fax machine, he arranges to send the company a brochure detailing the features of his particular machines and to call back in a few days.

The presentation call

This is the follow-up to the canvassing call and is made after the customer has received the relevant product information. During this call, the salesperson tries to achieve the following:

To clarify the needs of the customer

Although he will have already touched on this subject during his canvassing call, he must now deal with it in greater detail. He must discover precisely what the customer needs in order to run his business efficiently.

Example

In the example just given, the fax machine salesperson will try to establish precisely what sort of workload the customer has, how much paperwork needs to be sent out, whether this paperwork needs to be reproduced in colour, how vital this paperwork is to the company's business, and so forth. In other words, he will try to discover what the customer needs in order to run his business as efficiently as possible.

To match the benefits of his product to these customer needs

Having ascertained the needs of the customer, the salesperson now gives a clear presentation of his product – ie, what it can do and, more importantly, how it will satisfy the needs of the customer.

Example

The fax machine sales person will explain what his fax machines can do, how reliable and efficient they are, how cost-effective they are and so on. In short, he will try to make clear to the customer that his fax machines can be safely relied upon to solve all his (the customer's) problems of transmitting documents and other paperwork.

To handle any objections which the customer may have
Naturally, after hearing the salesperson explain the benefits of his product, the customer may still not be totally satisfied. He may, for example, object to the price of the product or its reliability. He may already have a supplier for the product in question and may be loath to take on a new supplier. These are all typical objections and the sales-person must be able to overcome them, or at least reassure the customer that the product is worth taking a risk with.

Example
In the fax machine case, the customer may object to buying his equip-ment from a small local company. He may tell the salesperson that he is worried about dealing with such a company – in case it goes bust or is otherwise unable to repair the machines it sells. In reply, the sales person must reassure the customer that, at the very least, such eventualities are highly unlikely. It may be, however, that the customer remains uncon-vinced.

To close the deal, or else clarify the objection
This is the final and most difficult stage of the call.

After dealing briefly with any immediate objections that the customer raises, the salesperson must now suggest that the customer buys the product. The process of 'asking' or 'suggesting' to a customer that he should buy something is known throughout the sales world as 'closing'.

As you might expect, the customer will usually react to this suggestion in one of three ways, as follows:

'Yes, I'll buy the product'
This is the least common reply, if only because most buyers prefer to take a little more time over spending their money with a comparative stranger. Nevertheless, if the customer does say 'Yes' at this stage, the salesperson must be prepared to take the order.

'I'll have to think about it'
Other variations of this type of reply include, 'I'll have to talk it over with my partner', or, 'I'm not going to decide today, call me in a couple of days', and so on.

This is the most common reply and it can mean anything from, 'I'm not in the least bit interested but I daren't say no to your face. With luck, you will now go away and stop bothering me', to, 'I like what I hear, but I need a day or so to adjust to the idea of spending money with you.'

In other words, it can be a qualified 'Yes', a 'No' or a 'Maybe'. The first thing a salesperson must do in reply is to try to discover which of these is nearest to the truth. This is normally done by asking one or two carefully chosen questions to clarify matters. (For further details, see Chapter 8.)

'Thanks, but no thanks'
This is also a fairly common reply. In this case, the salesperson tries to clarify the real reason for the 'No'.

This is easy to do in some cases, almost impossible in others, since it depends upon the tolerance and reasonableness of the customer in question. In any event, the salesperson's aim should be to clarify the reason behind the 'No' and to arrange to contact the buyer again as soon as possible, in order to discuss how this objection can be overcome.

Example
In the case of our brave fax machine salesperson, who has been told, 'Thanks, but no thanks, we don't want to buy from a small company like yours', he must check that he is being told the true reason for the 'No'. Once he has reassured himself that the small size of the company is indeed the real reason, he should arrange to ring back as soon as possible 'to see whether we can't get round this problem'. He should then discuss the matter with his own sales manager to see what can be done to change the customer's mind.

The closing call

Most customers do not immediately say 'Yes' when you ask them to buy your product at the end of your presentation call. Consequently, a third call to close the deal is required. This is a normal occurrence. Indeed, sometimes four or even five calls are required before all objections are overcome.

The aim of the closing call is to complete the deal and get the customer to buy the product. In nearly all cases, this involves overcoming a particular objection or series of objections and then asking the customer to buy.

Example
Our fax machine salesperson may give the customer details of other reputable companies who have purchased machines from him recently. By doing this, he hopes to convince the customer that other, perhaps larger, companies do not share his worries about buying from a small company. He may even offer an attractive discount on the normal price so as to reassure the customer into thinking, 'OK, at that price it's worth taking a risk'. Finally, he will propose to the customer that the deal be approved.

In all cases, where the customer chooses not to go ahead with the deal when asked, the salesman must repeat the clarification process which I referred to at the end of the presentation call and re-enter a new closing phase.

3. What to Do Before Picking Up the Phone

Nothing annoys a customer more than having to listen to a salesperson who does not know his facts or who seems disorganized. So, whatever you do, never pick up the phone to make a sales call before you are prepared for it.

There are basically two sorts of preparation: product preparation and daily preparation.

Product preparation

Chapter 1 referred briefly to company sales scripts. These are written scripts, which are sometimes given to new salespeople to help them talk to customers. They list the good points of the product in question, suggest ways of explaining them and so on. Unfortunately, in my experience, these scripts are usually inadequate for their purpose and so most salespeople generally have to prepare and arm themselves with the requisite product knowledge.

Whatever you are selling, whether it is a product or a service, you must do your best to know it inside out. To be specific, you must know (1) the facts of the product and (2) the benefits of the product.

The facts of the product
These include the features of the product, its performance, reliability and cost, details of the supplier and all details regarding after-sales service.

Example
Imagine you are selling a range of sticky tapes to hardware shops. Here are a few examples of the product facts you should know:

1. The exact type of tapes which your range includes (eg, Sellotape, insulating tape, heavy duty tape, double-sided tape).
2. What these tapes can be used for (eg, sticking paper, sticking other items, covering electrical connections, wrapping parcels, affixing things to walls).
3. Their size and dimensions (eg, the width of the tape, the length of the roll).
4. Their colours.
5. Their additional features (eg, automatic snap-off facility, transparency, whether waterproof).
6. Their containers and packaging (eg, whether they come in a box, a tin, or plain cellophane wrapping, whether they are packed individually or in twos, sixes, twelves).
7. Their price:

   - their individual recommended retail price to the consumer;
   - their individual price to the shop;
   - their individual price to the shop if ordered in large quantities.

8. The minimum quantity of tapes the shop must order.
9. The method and times of delivery of tapes that are ordered.
10. When the shop must pay for the tapes.
11. What credit terms are available.
12. How the shop should return faulty products for a refund.
13. Whether and how the shop can return unsold tapes for a refund.
14. Whether there is any point of sale material to go with the tapes (eg, shelf stickers, wall posters, window posters, special containers).
15. Whether the tapes are to be promoted or advertised to the consumer (eg, in magazines, newspapers, on local radio, tv).
16. Whether the tapes are very popular with shops and in the market generally.
17. The names of any local or national shops who already buy these tapes from you.

In addition you should know about the market position and the general sales of the company for whom you are selling these tapes. So, for example, you should know:

18. How long the company has been trading.
19. What its general business is. Perhaps it supplies many other products apart from sticky tape.
20. What its market position is. Is it a local, national or international company? Is it a major supplier of sticky tape? Where does it stand in relation to its competitors? Does it supply any/many other customers? Are any/many of its customers well known?
21. Whether it has any special trading conditions (eg, do all goods remain the property of the company until they are paid for? Do

queries or complaints about lost or faulty deliveries have to be notified to the company within a certain time?)

Lastly, you should be familiar with what sorts of sticky tape are generally being sold by your competitors, and how their service compares with yours. So, for example, you should know:

22. What sticky tapes your competitors sell.
23. How the popularity of their tapes compares with yours.
24. How their quality and price compare with yours.
25. How their delivery and service compare with yours.

There is quite a lot of information here, as you can see, but it is all important and relevant both to the product you are selling and to the customer to whom you are selling it.

And you must know it all. Ideally, you should memorize it, but if that is not possible (because, for example, the product is more complicated than sticky tape), then you should, at least, write it down and have it available at your fingertips.

The benefits of the product
Warning: Although you must know the facts of your product, you must now be able to turn these facts into benefits. Why? Because customers never buy products because of the facts about those products. Customers buy products because of the *benefits* those products will bring them.

Example
A hardware shop owner will not buy ten rolls of multi-purpose sticky tape simply because the tape in question can perform many tasks. He buys it because, by being multi-purpose, the tape is easier to sell to his customers. Whatever they want to use it for, he can say, 'That's the one you need.' The tape will, therefore, sell faster and it will make a faster profit for the shop owner.

So if you are selling a type of sticky tape that is multi-purpose, instead of pushing the fact it is multi-purpose, you push the benefit of faster sales and faster profits.

Here are some more examples of what I mean:

Suppose you are working for a small local supplier of stationery products. It is your job to telephone all the other companies in the area to sell them a range of paper, envelopes, pens, typewriters, typewriter equipment, adding machines, filing trays etc. The fact that you are local will not make anyone buy products from you, but the benefit of fast and attentive service – preventing the customer from having to waste money on large stocks of stationery – might.

Suppose you are selling Italian spaghetti (called 'Milano') for a London-based importer of Italian food products. It is your job to telephone the head buyers of all the major food stores such as Sainsburys, Tesco and Fine Fare to sell them this spaghetti. Instead of selling the fact that your spaghetti is Italian, and that it has an obviously Italian name like 'Milano', you should sell the benefit that because Italians are renowned for their spaghetti, British food shoppers are more likely to buy a brand that is unmistakably Italian.

Suppose you are working for a large taxi company. It is your job to telephone other local companies to persuade them to use your taxi service whenever they require transport. The fact that your company is large and owns a huge fleet of taxis will not persuade companies to use your service. However, what might convince them is the benefit of using a taxi company that can always guarantee them a spare car and thus save them time and money keeping staff and customers waiting.

Suppose you are working for a Birmingham company that specializes in importing toy cars from Malaysia. It is your job to sell these toys to toyshops, department stores and garages throughout the UK. Let us also suppose that the price you are offering them at is one of the lowest in the market, for that type of toy. Instead of selling the fact that these toy cars are cheap and will not, therefore, cost your customers a great deal, you should sell the benefit that most kids and most parents are likely to snap them up because they cost so little. This will mean faster sales and faster profits for the shop that stocks them.

The moral: When you explain the facts of your product to a customer, make quite sure that you go on to answer the implicit question, 'So what?' Tell him the benefits that he will receive if he buys the product. Remember, people buy things for their benefits (for what these things will do for them) not for their particular features or facts.

Listing your benefits

I hope that, after reading the section on the facts of the product (see p 18), you have written out a list of product facts that you have either memorized or kept for reference.

What you must now do is to look carefully at each of your product facts and, in each case, ask yourself the question 'So what?' What good is this fact to the customer? What benefit can he expect to receive from this fact?

I suggest that you take a sheet of paper and on one side write down your facts and on the other write down your benefits. Here are a few more examples of how certain facts give rise to certain benefits. (Words in brackets are added for explanation only.)

Fact	*Benefit*
(You are selling sticky tape to shops.) Your tape can be delivered within 48 hours.	Customer needs to order in small amounts, thus keeping his stock bill down to a minimum. (Saves money.)
(You are selling spaghetti to food stores.) Your spaghetti comes in bright red packets.	Customer's shoppers will notice product more easily. This will lead to better brand awareness and faster sales. (Faster profits.)
(You are selling office furniture to companies.) Your furniture is of very high quality.	Companies who buy it will 'look good', impress their customers and get more sales. (Extra sales.)
(You are selling a new brand of beer to pubs.) TV adverts will soon appear for this beer.	Drinkers will see the adverts and will then want to buy the beer. (Extra sales.)
(You are selling sunglasses to chemists.) They are made of plastic.	Shop's customers will save money because plastic is durable, long-lasting and no danger to them from broken glass. (Easier to sell and faster sales.)
(You are selling exhibition space to companies.) The exhibition is being held on a bank holiday.	Exhibitors can expect more people to visit the exhibition because most will have the day off. (Better chance of sales.)
(You sell microwaves to cafés.) They cook hot snacks in 90 seconds.	Customers get faster service. More customers can be served at lunchtime. Fewer staff are needed to serve them. (Happier customers, more sales and lower costs.)
Your company is one of the biggest in the market.	Customer is dealing with a reliable no-risk company with a proven track record. (Reliability.)
Your company is small.	Customer will receive better, more attentive service. (Better service.)
Your products are among the most expensive on the market.	Customer is paying for reliability and quality performance. After all, you only get what you pay for. (Reliability and quality.)

Fact	*Benefit*
Your products are cheaper than most.	Customer is getting value for money. (Extra profits.)
(You are selling to shops.) Your product is heavily advertised.	Shop's customers will recognize the brand and buy it in preference to others. (Better chance of sales.)
Your product is not advertised at all.	Customer is not paying for expensive advertising and therefore gets better value. (Extra profits.)
Your product is made in Britain.	Customer's orders are less prone to transportation problems and/or currency fluctuations. (More reliability.)
Your product is bought by customer's rivals.	If similar companies use it, it must be good. (Reliability.)

These are some examples of how to derive benefits from facts. It is not difficult and you should not have any difficulty with your own list, but if you do, ask for advice. Ask your sales manager, if you have one. That is what he is there for! If you have no one to turn to, just concentrate on asking yourself 'So what?' after each fact, and you will soon get the hang of it.

Assuming that you now have a list of both your product facts and your product benefits, your product preparation is nearly complete. All that remains is for you to try to commit all this information to memory. It may be a nuisance but, believe me, it will be worth it. Nothing impresses a customer more than a salesperson who knows his stuff, and, by the same token, nothing turns him off faster than a salesperson who does not. So don't risk being found out. Know your product and be successful!

Daily preparation

Usual sales office procedure
When you start selling, you are usually given three sales aids to help you in your work.

● First, you will be given a number of *customer record cards*. These contain details of individual customers (their address/phone number/contact name/the last occasion they were spoken to/what they have bought – if anything – and when). They are customers who are known to your company and who have already been approached.

- Second, you will probably also be given cards or sheets of paper containing the names of other companies who have not been approached. These are your *cold customer cards*, for want of a better expression. Details of these companies are likely to be sparse and will probably amount to no more than name, address and (possibly) a telephone number. These two different groups of customers represent your *sales leads* and it will be your job to maintain sales contact with the first group and open contact with the second.
- Third, you will usually (but not always) be given some form of *desk diary* to help you plan your daily routine.

Now let's see how you can make use of these and other sales aids.

Take charge of your own preparation and planning
When you are selling, it is vital that you plan your day and prepare the calls that you intend to make. For the sake of simplicity, this personal organization may be divided as follows.

Make a daily call list
Try to make sure that you get into the habit of writing out a daily list of the people you intend to call. You will find this list extremely valuable because talking to dozens of strangers on the telephone can be an arduous experience. Certain calls can leave you dispirited, distracted and most unenthusiastic when it comes to redialling yet another customer.

In order to counter this natural weariness, it is vital to maintain some sort of momentum and a steady rate of calls. In other words, you must always know who you are going to call *next*.

The best way of achieving this is to have *one single written list* containing the name, telephone number and contact name of each company you wish to call.

Where this list includes companies on whom you also have a customer record card, you should, of course, have this card to hand, in case it contains helpful information, but you should basically work from your list and not from a pile of cards.

One final point: make sure that your daily call list contains the telephone numbers of all the companies on it. If you do not know them, spend half an hour getting hold of them *before* you start selling. Otherwise, your momentum will be completely disrupted every time you come to a company name without a number.

The best time to write your daily call list is either last thing the previous evening for first thing in the morning. Get into this habit when you first start selling and you will not regret it.

Write things down
With all this talk of customer record cards, sheets of sales leads, daily

lists and so on, you are probably thinking, 'Oh dear, it all sounds a bit complicated'. You are right! Selling does (unfortunately) involve a fair amount of record-keeping and general paperwork. Few salespeople enjoy it, but none can afford to ignore it.

My advice is to get it under control when you start selling. Then, instead of it being a nuisance, it will actually help to make life easier and increase your sales. Writing things down is an important factor in this process of taking control. Even the best memory is useless in comparison with the written word.

Customer record cards

These cards play a vital role in any sales office. They are usually the only source of detailed information on the companies concerned. You must make sure that you keep them up to date. It also pays to record your sales conversations with customers in some detail. Jotting down the fact that the customer places a premium on reliability or cost, or does not like being phoned first thing in the morning, or even the fact that he supports Manchester United, may be a deciding factor in clinching a future sale.

Desk diaries

A desk diary is a salesperson's best friend. If you are not given one, buy one; you cannot sell properly without one.

Ideally, if the diary is big enough, use it to record your daily call list. That way, all your calls will be located in one place.

The principal function of your desk diary, however, is to enable you to keep a note of your call backs. For example, one company whom you telephone may be permanently engaged, so make a note to call back at a different time of the day. Another company may be using an answer-phone or may have closed early, so once again make a note to call back. Most of your call backs will be because the person you want to speak to is unavailable (busy or out of the office) or (if you do speak to him) because he has to discuss your sales proposition with his colleagues or wait for your product information to arrive.

In all cases, make sure that you have a written note of who to call back, the name and telephone number of his company and the time the call is to be made. Incidentally, these calls back should be the first series of calls to be written down on your daily call list.

Plan your day

When you are selling over the telephone, your normal day will probably include most or all of the following:

- Finding out the telephone numbers of companies for whom you have an address only.
- Finding out the individual name of the person you have to speak to at a particular company.

- Making canvassing calls to customers.
- Making presentation calls to customers.
- Making closing calls to customers.
- Dealing with problems that have occurred.

All these calls require a different approach, a slightly different level of commitment from you when you make them. Calling Directory Enquiries for telephone numbers, for example, is clearly nothing like as arduous as closing a sale. In other words, even though you must be reasonably alert during all your calls, some of them require you to be especially clear-headed and fluent. You must organize your day accordingly.

Here are two simple rules which you may find useful:

Make difficult calls when you feel good
This is self-explanatory. If the first hour in the day is a nightmare for you, then use it to find out your telephone numbers and contact names. There again, if you feel especially good in the mid-morning and late afternoon, use these times to deal with any difficult problems and to close sales. Of course, the precise time you speak to your customers will largely depend upon their availability, not your personal preference. Nevertheless, there is no sense in not trying to put your good periods to best use.

Make your calls work for you
In practice, different types of sales call require you to say different things.

Canvassing calls, for example, require you to introduce yourself and your company quickly and clearly. You will probably even use a similar form of words for each call. Likewise, presentation calls; and even if they vary a little more than canvassing calls, they still require you to explain similar things in each case.

As a result, organize your daily call list so that you make a series of the same type of call one after the other. Spend an hour, for example, making just canvassing calls; because you have to say similar things in each call you will find yourself becoming more fluent with each call. By using this process, you are making your calls work for you.

In addition, when it comes to deciding which companies to canvass or which companies to make your presentation calls to, try telephoning a series of similar types of company. So, for example, if you selling advertising for a local newspaper, concentrate on just canvassing car dealers or alternatively just electrical shops. By repeatedly calling the same type of company, you will quickly familiarize yourself with the typical attitudes and concerns of such a company and improve your handling of it accordingly. Once again, you are making your calls work for you.

Planning calls to specific customers

Even if you have planned when to call a particular customer and even if your product knowledge is immaculate, you may still have to plan part of the call in advance.

For example, you may know in advance that the customer is going to ask a particular question or is likely to raise a particular issue. You may, therefore, have to prepare what you are going to say in reply.

Likewise, in order to make the best possible impression on a customer whom you are calling for the first time, it may help you to read through one of his company's advertisements or brochures before dialling. Then, when you pick up the phone and speak to the customer, you will be able to demonstrate how knowledgeable you are about his business. This is bound to create a good impression with your listener.

There are lots of similar situations where a call (or part of a call) requires preparation in order to make it fully effective. Try and be aware of this and make a point of scrutinizing your daily call list for any calls that may require this treatment.

Conclusion: Increase your preparation and increase your sales

Sales preparation, that is preparing your product knowledge and preparing your day, is one of the key factors in sales achievement.

Unfortunately, too many salespeople fail to recognize its importance and suffer accordingly. Their product knowledge is slipshod, their work days are filled with a hotchpotch of unplanned calls to a mixed bag of customers: even their desks and files are disorganized and untidy. The result is that, all too often, their lack of preparation and organization leads to a lack of sales.

You, on the other hand, should aim to be prepared and organized at all times. This means constantly making an effort every day of your sales career to maintain your daily call list, your diary and your general record-keeping. It also means that you will increase your sales.

4. Practical Advice about How to Talk on the Telephone

This chapter deals with a few important principles that you must adopt when speaking to customers. They must become second nature to you.

None of them are difficult to understand but they will need rehearsing before you become fully familiar with them. So learn them and rehearse them before you put them into practice.

If it helps, try to write out an imaginary script for yourself and your product, using the principles contained in this chapter. Then recite it out loud or role-play the situation with a colleague.

This technique of writing scripts and/or role playing with another person is a very useful way of improving your sales technique, so, if you have not tried it before, do not be put off because it all sounds a bit silly. It is usually a great help.

Speak slowly and clearly and avoid jargon

Nearly everyone who receives an unexpected phone call from a stranger takes at least ten seconds to adjust to what is being said. This does not mean that they are stupid, it is simply that they need time to 'wake up' to what is going on.

After this initial 'wake up' period – during which, incidentally, they remember practically nothing that is said to them – they gradually start listening, and usually, after another ten seconds or so, they become fully alert.

This applies in business as much as it does in ordinary life.

So remember, when telephoning a customer who has not spoken to you before, or who does not know you very well, give him time to adjust to who you are and where you are calling from.

The best way to help your listener adjust is to speak slowly, speak clearly and avoid jargon.

Speak slowly

There is a perfectly natural tendency to talk fast when we are telephoning a customer for the first time. We probably feel that we have to get our first few words out as quickly as possible or else our listener will hang up. You must try to resist this temptation – no one is going to hang up on you!

Instead, try to speak as slowly as you dare (without sounding ridiculous) for the first 20 seconds of your call.

A useful technique in this situation is to use two or three words where you would normally only use one!

For example, if you are selling advertising space to local companies, you might be tempted to introduce yourself like this:

'Hello, it's John Smith from the *Evening Post*.'

On the face of it, this introduction sounds perfectly OK: it's short and sharp and to the point. The problem is that, even if you say it very slowly, it still only takes three to seven seconds from start to finish. As a result, your customer will not have been able to adjust to you in that time and will probably (at best) simply ask you to repeat yourself or (at worst) be totally confused.

In order to avoid this, try extending your introduction by adding a few extra words, like this:

'Hello. I don't think that we have spoken together before. My name is John Smith. I work for X Publishing Ltd. We publish the *Evening Post* newspaper.'

This takes about 14 seconds to say, or slightly longer if you can manage to linger on the words 'before' and 'Smith'. The point is that, by taking 14 seconds to say something that could really have been said in three to seven seconds, you have given your listener time to gradually 'wake up' to who you are and where you are from. He is, therefore, ready and able to receive the next part of your call and you have successfully negotiated your first hurdle.

Here is another pair of examples, with their respective times in brackets.

'Hello. It's John Smith from Amazing Cards Ltd, the greetings card company.' (10 seconds)

'Hello. I don't think we have spoken together before. My name is John Smith. I work for Amazing Cards Ltd. We print a wide range of greetings cards – Christmas cards, birthday cards, cards for special occasions, you know, that sort of thing.' (about 20 seconds)

Once again, by adopting a more wordy introduction you have allowed your listener to gradually 'wake up' to what is happening.

Try to practise this technique. It may seem strange at first, especially if you have not sold before, but you will soon get the hang of it.

Speak clearly

This is both obvious and self-explanatory but it still needs saying. Too many salespeople are oblivious to the importance of treating their listeners as carefully as possible.

Remember, not everyone has perfect hearing, not everyone can understand certain accents and not everyone is familiar with the sort of informal slang that you use with friends. Try to make a point of holding the telephone receiver properly and speak *into* it rather than across it. It is little points like these that help to create the right or the wrong impression at the other end of the phone.

Avoid jargon and complicated language

Always use simple words and phrases when speaking on the telephone. Clarity always takes precedence over slickness when it comes to sales talk.

For example, it may sound more impressive to say:

'I'm the senior chain-store representative for Golden Corn Milling Division.'

But it is much clearer and, therefore, more effective, to say:

'I work for Golden Corn. I'm in charge of selling bread to all the large shops.'

Be simple, be clear and be effective.

Explain things by painting verbal pictures

People always find it more difficult to grasp things over the telephone than they do face-to-face. Words alone, without gestures, rarely seem to be able to capture their interest and imagination.

In addition, most company buyers listen to dozens of different salespeople every week, so it is hardly surprising that the attention span of these buyers becomes shorter and shorter – as does their capacity to become 'interested' in what salespeople have to say.

To make the best of this difficult situation, try to capture the interest of your listener by painting verbal pictures for him, when you explain your product.

Example

Imagine you are working for a recruitment agency. Your job is to telephone company directors to persuade them to use your agency to fill their staff vacancies. When one of these directors asks you why his company should use your agency, you might say something like this:

> 'Well, there are a number of reasons why you should let us handle your staff recruitment. First, we can save you valuable time. For example, whenever you need to fill a vacancy, simply contact our office, explain your requirements and we will see to all the details. We will advertise the vacancy confidentially in the local press, we will interview all suitable applicants, check their references and draw up a shortlist. Then, depending on what you prefer, we will either appoint someone to the vacancy ourselves or arrange for you to interview the shortlist candidates yourself and then make the final selection. The whole process takes only ten days.
>
> Second, because we take care of all these details, we save you money. Not only will you be able to concentrate on your own business affairs while all this is going on, but also, if the person selected for the job does not live up to your expectations, we'll replace them free of charge. Now how does that sound?'

This is all perfectly adequate and informative, but it sounds a bit lifeless and uninteresting. A better approach is to try painting a verbal picture of your product, like this:

> 'The reason you should use us is because we make life easier for you. After all, you know how exasperating looking for staff can be.
>
> First, you will probably have to advertise the vacancy, which might mean announcing to your rivals and customers that you are short-staffed. Then, as soon as the advert appears, you have to organize people to answer the telephone, hold the interviews, make the shortlist, do the final interviews and so on. Even when you do give the job to someone, you can still get your fingers burned. Either their references don't check out or they don't hit it off with other people in the office or they suddenly leave because they have been offered more money elsewhere. Whatever the problem, you are back to square one and the whole process has to be repeated all over again.
>
> 'However, if you let *us* find your staff for you, all these problems are avoided and you'll have exactly the sort of person you are looking for, in your office within ten days. Now how does that sound?'

Read both these examples carefully and study their differences.

First, compare the general approach that each takes. The first concentrates on presenting a straightforward account of what the agency can do for the customer and how he will benefit. As I said, it is informative but it suffers from one major defect: it sounds lifeless. And it sounds lifeless because the situation it describes *is* lifeless.

By contrast, the second version focuses on the frustration of looking for staff. The situation it describes sounds more interesting because it *is*. Remember: as a salesperson, it is your job to interest the customer as well as inform him, so try to be creative when you explain your product. Try painting a verbal picture.

Second, compare the actual language used in each of these different versions. In the second one, for example, look at these particular words and phrases:

'make life easier'
'exasperating'
'rivals'
'short-staffed'
'you can still get your fingers burned'
'don't hit it off'
'you are back to square one'
'exactly the sort of person you are looking for'
'in your office'

I am sure you agree that all these words and phrases conjure up fairly strong images. They mean something to the listener. Now look at the language used in our first version:

'valuable time'
'explain your requirements'
'we will see to all the details'
'confidentially'
'make the final selection'
'the whole process only takes ten days'
'we save you money'
'concentrate on your own business affairs'
'does not live up to your expectations'

All these words and phrases may be useful and informative but they are not evocative – they do not create the sort of strong images that are likely to maintain someone's interest and attention. The lesson is, use language that means something to your customer. Use words and phrases that are more lifelike and more likely to arouse interest. Think of them as the colours in your verbal picture.

Example
Imagine you are selling advertising space, in a local newspaper, to restaurants. Let us say you are trying to sell a particular proprietor an advert which includes a colour photo of his restaurant. Let us also assume that the cost is one-third of his small ad in the *Yellow Pages*.

How do you overcome the customer's objection that your product simply does not compare with the *Yellow Pages*? Do you, for example, quote comparative circulation and readership statistics or cite a mass of comparative reader-response data? Do you mention the fact that newspaper advertising is often more up to date than that of the *Yellow Pages*, and so on?

Possibly, but not to begin with.

The first thing that you must do is to grab the attention of your listener by painting a verbal picture of the message you want to get across. So try something like this:

> 'OK, Mr Smith, suppose that someone wants to take his family out for a meal. How does he go about deciding where to go, assuming that he wants to try somewhere different? He might, as you say, use his *Yellow Pages*. He might turn to the "Restaurant" section and go through the 500 or so restaurants listed and he might, after going through all the ads and all the fine print, pick out yours. He might, but it's not very likely, is it? Not only are the odds against it, but what is he going to see in your ad that is going to make such a big impression on him? After all, your ad probably says pretty much the same as dozens and dozens of others. So why choose yours?
>
> 'In any case, is that really how people choose where to eat? Don't they usually want to know something about the look of the place, something about its atmosphere and so on? I mean, wouldn't it make more sense to have a nice photograph of the inside of your restaurant splashed across our "Where to Eat" section? That way, people could see what sort of a place you have. And some of them are going to say "Hmmm, that looks nice, why don't we try there?"'

Do you see what I am getting at? By painting a real-life scene, you are helping to make your message come alive.

Practice makes perfect

Painting verbal pictures is an important technique for explaining things over the phone. However, it needs practice!

Here are some suggestions for how you might be able to speed up the process:

- Practise writing out a series of scripts for yourself, which paint verbal pictures of key points that you wish to make about your product.
- Get to know more about your customers and the situations in which they can use your product. Use these facts in your verbal pictures.
- Try to envisage practical situations in which a customer might not have your product and might, therefore, be at a disadvantage. Again, use specific details from these situations to enliven your verbal pictures.

● Always check that you are presenting your product and explaining its benefits in the most interesting and imaginative way. Do not be content to simply repeat the old phrases time and time again. Be interesting and be effective.

When and how to ask questions

Like most of the skills and techniques that are used by salespeople, knowing when and how to ask questions is more of an art than a science. Nevertheless, one or two simple, practical points are worth mentioning.

The difference between open and closed questions
All questions can be divided into two types: open and closed.

Open questions
These are questions which *cannot* be answered 'Yes' or 'No'. They require a fuller reply. Open questions typically begin with words like Why, What, Where, Which, Who and How. Examples of open questions are:

'What sort of food shopper do you get in your shop?'
'Why not use colour in your packaging?'
'Where do you advertise at the moment?'
'Which area is the most important for you?'
'Who generally has the final say?'
'How would you normally handle that?'
'When do you normally sell the most?'

As you can see, none of these questions can be properly answered with a simple 'Yes' or 'No': they all require more information from the person who answers.

Closed questions
Closed questions are ones that can be answered with a simple 'Yes' or 'No'. Examples of closed questions are:

'Are you in charge of marketing?'
'Has your budget been spent?'
'Do you see what I am getting at?'
'Are you telling me that the official policy of your company is to buy only from public companies who have been trading for more than ten years?'
'Can you think of any example of when you might need a fax machine, Mr Smith, say, any time over the next few months?'
'Are you busy?'

As you can see, the length of the question makes no difference to whether it can be answered 'Yes' or 'No'.

Concentrate on asking open questions

Open questions are useful little things to have up your sleeve, especially in the following situations:

When you want to find out about a company

For example, take the situation when you canvass a company whom you have never contacted before. As we have seen, one of the aims of such a canvassing call is to find out more about the company, what it does, how it does it and so on. This is most easily achieved by asking relevant open questions.

So if you are selling a range of pet foods to pet shops, for example, you might ask:

'What sorts of pet do you cater for exactly?'
'Roughly how big is your shop?'
'How close are you to the town centre?'
'How are you finding business overall?'
'To what extent do you prefer dealing with distributors?'
'When is the best time to get hold of you on the phone?'

As you can see, these open questions are difficult for your listener to avoid. As a result, they usually get the information you require.

When you wish to establish the precise needs of the customer

As I mentioned earlier, you follow up your initial canvassing call with your presentation call. The first aim of this presentation call is to establish the *precise needs* of the customer, so as to be able to match these needs with the benefits of your product. Once again, this is best achieved with open questions, such as:

'What types of pet account for most of your business?'
'What sorts of pet food do you stock for them?'
'How many flavours do you stock?'
'How is your pet food packaged?'
'How often do you have to reorder?'
'What sort of price do you pay for it, if you don't mind my asking?'
How long have you been dealing with your suppliers?'
'How important is price to you when it comes to buying?'

These open questions enable you politely to probe the customer for specific information.

When you want to prolong the conversation in order to get to know the customer a little better

As we shall see in the next chapter, it is very important to remember that all customers are human beings first and business people second. Getting to know the personal side of the buyer you speak to is, therefore, very helpful in all sorts of ways. So, for example, if you get a suitable opportunity you might ask:

'How on earth did you get into this sort of business, Mr Smith?'
'How does it compare with what you were doing before?'
'What sort of problems normally get dumped in your lap?'
'How on earth do you manage to cope with everything?'
'What's your company like to work for?'

When your customer 'throws' you off-balance
You are bound to experience situations in which a customer throws you with an awkward or unexpected comment (see p 65). Having one or two open questions up your sleeve, to ask in this situation, can often help you to maintain your poise and retain the initiative.

For example, if you are thrown by a sudden objection to your product, try asking:

'In what way do you mean that, Mr Brown?'
'What makes you think that, Mr Smith?'
Which particular aspect are you referring to, Mr Jones?'
'How reasonable is that, Mr Bloggs?'
What supplier can honestly guarantee that, Mr Green?'

By preparing this sort of defensive open question in advance, you can often throw the ball back at the customer, and give yourself time to rearrange your thoughts.

Be careful when asking closed questions
Except when you are talking about relatively unimportant issues, be very careful when asking closed questions. The reason is that they can backfire on you, by allowing the customer to deny you information or duck the question entirely.

Example
If you were to ask, 'Does your shop mainly cater for dogs and cats?', your listener might respond simply 'No', without volunteering any further information. You would, therefore, be forced to ask another question to clarify your first question and you would lose the initiative in the process. However, if you had asked, 'What sorts of pet do you cater for exactly?', you would not have had this problem.

Example
You want to arrange to call your customer back in a couple of days. You could ask, 'Can I call you back on Friday?' However, to avoid him simply saying 'No', try asking, 'I'd like to call you back in a couple of days, how does Friday sound?' In this case, even if the customer does object, he will probably feel obliged to suggest an alternative date and you will have retained the initiative.

Permissible closed questions
You cannot avoid asking closed questions altogether. It is just not possible. There will be several occasions, during your sales calls, when you will have to ask your listener what he thinks about something. In other words, you want a direct answer.

In such a situation you must try to phrase your question so that – even though it is technically closed – it cannot easily be answered in a negative or disruptive way.

Example
After you have told your buyer about the benefits of your recruitment agency, you should not ask, 'Are you impressed, Mr Smith?' That simply invites a 'No' or a 'Not really'. Instead, you should put your question a little more positively. Something like, 'Now isn't that the sort of service you're looking for, Mr Smith?', or 'Now that's not bad, is it?', or 'Now, you've got to admit that's an interesting proposition, isn't it, Mr Smith?'

In other words, put your question in such a way that only an unreasonable person would answer 'No', the point being that most people who do answer 'No' to such a question will feel obliged to go on to explain why, and if by chance they do not, you can immediately jump in and ask them why they said 'No'. In either case, you will find that you retain the initiative and avoid the problem of being 'thrown'.

Answering a question with a question
Occasionally, when selling to a customer on the phone, you will be asked for information (eg, your price) which you are not yet ready to give. In such a situation, try using an open question of your own to parry the customer's enquiry and at the same time to further your presentation.

Example

Salesperson: We actually specialize in dog food . . . .

Customer [interrupting]: Yes, but what's your price?

Salesperson: It really depends on how much you order. How many tins did you have in mind?

Here you have parried the question and asked one of your own in order to move on with your sales presentation.

Example

Salesperson: So as you can see, Mr Smith, the product seems to be getting more and more popular – with more and more shops switching to our brand.

Customer: Yes, but supposing I do buy from you and the product
              doesn't sell, can I send it back for a refund?

Salesperson: Under certain conditions, yes. But tell me, what makes
              you think that the product won't sell?

Once again, you have deflected an awkward question with one of your
own and, at the same time, you have begun to probe for customer
objections. You have definitely retained the initiative.

Conclusion
Whichever way you look at it, good questions are essential to good sales
calls. Unfortunately, they must be carefully thought out in advance. So
try not to be the sort of salesperson who flounders for want of a good
question. As usual, be prepared and be effective.

5. Practical Advice about Dealing with Buyers on the Telephone

Three endemic problems

One of the first problems about selling to someone over the phone is that you cannot see who you are talking to and you cannot see his office environment. In effect, you are working blind.

Another problem is that most buyers make their decisions about whether and how much to buy when they are off the phone. So you are usually not privy to how they arrive at these decisions – be they favourable or unfavourable.

Finally, because so little of your time will be spent face-to-face with your customers, you will inevitably feel the temptation to treat them like the disembodied voices they are. Certainly, after ringing 100 companies, and speaking to maybe 50 buyers, one after the other, you will find it a great effort to think of these people as individual persons.

All these problems are unique to selling over the phone. They rarely affect travelling salespeople because the latter meet their customers face-to-face, and are often present at the crucial time when decisions are argued out and taken.

Nevertheless, you must try not to allow the fact that you are selling blind to a series of voices to affect your sales. Instead, you must develop ways and means of overcoming it.

With this aim in mind, try observing the following principles and rules, or at least try to have them in the back of your mind for when you speak to your fiftieth buyer of the day!

Remember that all buyers are under invisible pressure

All buyers, whether they are managing directors, sales directors, marketing directors, production managers, purchasing managers or just middle-ranking executives, are usually under some sort of pressure.

They might be sitting in crowded, uncomfortable offices. They might be in a meeting or in the middle of a crisis. They might be desperate to meet a particular deadline. They might be waiting for an important visitor or an urgent telephone call. They might be anxious to go to the bathroom or to leave work early. They might be worried about their job, their health or their personal life. They might be preoccupied with pleasing their boss or with keeping their company afloat. They might even have just received a phone call from another salesperson who might have irritated or upset them and made them temporarily antagonistic towards similar callers.

This pressure can often make these buyers react negatively to salespeople. You must learn to recognize when this negative reaction is really this 'pressure' talking. This gives rise to our first rule for dealing with buyers.

Rule 1. Do not be too easily brushed off. Ask for a specific reason and, if necessary, ring back

Some concrete examples will demonstrate what I mean.

Suppose you are selling office furniture to local companies. You canvass six managing directors who, after listening briefly, give you the brush-off. All say after a few moments, 'Thanks, but no thanks'. Unfortunately, you have had a bad day and, in all cases, you fail to ask for a specific reason for their lack of interest. As a result, all six companies are marked down in your files as being 'Not interested'. However, if we were to go behind the scenes, as it were, we might discover some or all of the following.

Company 1

The MD was preparing for an important sales meeting and was in no mood to speak to anyone, especially someone trying to sell him something. He said 'Not interested' so he could return to his own, more pressing work, even though one of the items to be discussed in the sales meeting was 'equipping the new telephone sales office'.

Company 2

Here the MD had just received the sales figures for the previous month from his sales manager: they showed a big drop. He was in no mood to discuss spending any extra money at the time you called. Ironically, however, he had just told his sales manager to get the company reps to improve their sales presentation. So at the very moment you spoke to him, his sales manager was on the phone to one of your rival suppliers (of flip charts and other office accessories) ordering equipment to help improve these sales presentations.

Company 3

The MD said 'Not interested' because he was worried that the company's offices were already too small for the staff they employed without taking up more space with more furniture. He had more or less decided that the company would be moving into larger premises within a couple of months, without realizing of course, that he would need more furniture at that stage.

Company 4

In this case, the MD considered new furniture a luxury. He really did not see anything wrong with the furniture he had already; even though it was old, it was still perfectly solid. Having said that, he did not actually have a real objection to buying new furniture. Indeed, he might well have stopped to give the matter more thought if he had been told about how he could impress customers (and get more business) with a new office image. As it was, he was more concerned with clearing his desk so he could leave for his weekly game of golf.

Company 5

The MD did not usually deal with buying new furniture himself; he usually left it to his administration manager. However, the latter was on holiday when you rang and the MD could not be bothered to explain this fact.

Company 6

In this case, the personal assistant to the MD was off sick. As a result, the MD had just spent half an hour doing nothing but taking calls from a variety of salespeople. When you called, he had simply had enough. He said 'Not interested' without even being aware of, or interested in, what you were talking about.

These six examples are very common. The lesson they contain is that if you had very politely pushed for a specific reason for the lack of interest you encountered, you would probably have come away a wiser person and, who knows, you might even have been able to arrange to call back one or two of the MDs at a more convenient time, with more favourable results.

Sometimes you will not exactly be brushed off, but, instead, you will feel that your customer simply is not listening. If this happens and you feel that your listener is too preoccupied to give you his full attention, then politely suggest that you ring back at a more convenient time. In addition, even though in the heat of the moment it is not always easy, try to get the customer to specify a time for your call back. That way, you avoid a repetition of the situation.

The examples of companies 4, 5 and 6 illustrate this point perfectly.

Remember that buyers rarely buy alone
When it comes to spending money, we all like a little reassurance. We like to be told that what we intend to buy (and what we intend to pay for it) is 'OK'. And the more important the purchase and/or the higher the price, the more reassurance we need. All this applies equally in business, especially if the buyer lacks real authority within the company. So, after you have explained your product to a buyer and satisfied most of his objections, the chances are that he will then discuss your proposition with one of his colleagues.

This is when problems start to occur! Not only may this colleague have several *different* objections of his own, but also the buyer himself may forget one or two of the benefits of your product that you mentioned. Both these possibilities can lead to your proposition being severely mauled and even rejected during the course of this consultation. And this can happen, despite the fact that your buyer was himself very much in favour of the proposition at the time you spoke to him. How can you try to avoid this happening to you?

Rule 2. Give the buyer a watertight story
By this I mean: give the buyer a complete answer to all possible objections and check, before you ring off, that everything is clear in his mind. If you can send him a fax confirming some of the details which you have explained, so much the better.

Example
Suppose you are selling Russian-made boxes of matches to cash-and-carry stores and supermarkets. You speak to one buyer at one particular supermarket and he seems impressed, especially because your matches are much cheaper than the other British and European brands. Alas, you are so pleased that the low price seems to be swinging the deal in your favour, that you omit to arm the buyer with the answers to other objections. As a result, when the buyer discusses your proposition with a colleague, he is unable to counter this colleague's objection that Russian-made matches are unreliable and less popular than other European brands. Thus, when you ring the next morning to complete the transaction, you discover to your horror that the deal is off.

What should you have done?
You should have assumed that someone was going to raise the issue of where the matches were made. You would, therefore, have given your buyer the details of the latest market survey which showed that con-

sumers pay no attention to where matches are made. It also reveals that the reliability of Russian matches is on a par with most other European brands. Of course, if your buyer had had all this information to hand when he discussed the matter with his colleague, your proposition would have survived with flying colours.

The moral of the story is this: assume that all obvious objections are going to be raised by someone and arm your buyer with the answers accordingly. If necessary, raise an objection *for* him and then give him the answer. In short, give him a watertight story.

Remember that buyers are human beings

If this sounds too obvious, let me tell you that more salespeople fail because they forget this elementary principle than for any other reason, so please take it seriously.

What exactly am I getting at? Simply this: in ordinary everyday life, you automatically adjust what you say and how you say it to your particular listener. Take your friends, for example: the chances are that you are more restrained with those who are more serious-minded, less restrained and more casual with those who enjoy a good laugh. In the same way, you would almost certainly avoid being loud and frivolous with a friend who was feeling miserable and you certainly would not talk in a formal or impersonal way to your wife or husband!

Selling over the phone requires a similar adaptation and tact. You must try to develop a 'feel' for the person behind the voice, a 'feel' for what makes that person different from the others.

Rule 3. Listen for the individual at the other end of the telephone

Start listening immediately

Do not wait until you speak to the buyer himself before you start listening. You can start listening the moment your call is answered by the company receptionist. Give the name of the buyer you wish to speak to and *listen*. Sometimes the name will prompt a reaction: it might be a tone of respect, it might even be a chuckle.

Then, when you get through to the buyer's office, there may be other small signs of his personality and status. An older secretary or personal assistant is usually a sign that the buyer is older, more senior and sometimes a little more formal than usual; whereas a younger personal assistant is frequently a sign that the buyer is younger and perhaps less senior. In addition, how the personal assistant herself responds to you may be a sign of the person to come. For example, a frosty, somewhat stern personal assistant may well presage a boss with a similar personality; likewise the situation of a personal assistant who is more friendly and easy-going. And if this sounds too much like amateur psychology, let me tell you that you would be amazed at how often you can gauge the character of a buyer by talking to his secretary. So, *listen.*

Listen to the buyer him/herself
This is the difficult bit. Forming an accurate impression of someone merely by listening to them for a few moments on the phone is a hazardous business. It takes a great deal of experience and even then you can get it completely wrong. Still, you will get nowhere if you do not try. So, once again, *listen* carefully.

Listen to the tone of his voice, listen to how he refers to other members of the company, listen to how he responds to your product presentation and listen to how he puts his objections.

All these are important signs of the type of person behind the voice.

Find out more by asking questions
Do not be afraid to ask personal questions. The best time to do this is after you have finished the business part of your call, so try to hang on for a few moments and see what you can discover.

Questions about the buyer's personal business needs
No, this is not a contradiction in terms! These questions are asked in order to discover the buyer's personal thoughts about his job.

For example, if you are selling ink to a print manager working for a large printing company, ask him what he personally thinks is the most important thing about an ink, what he personally looks for when buying a new ink. It goes without saying that this sort of information is absolutely priceless.

Questions about the buyer's private interests
On a quieter note, it pays to find out a little about your buyer's individual interests and attitudes. Obviously, the way you go about this will vary with the circumstances and from buyer to buyer; however, you might ask him something like this:

> 'You sound as though you've been doing this for quite a while. How longer have you been with the company?'
> 'You've got quite a set-up there by the sound of it. Tell me, how on earth do you manage to cope with it all?'
> 'Have you got a busy weekend ahead of you, or are you just going to put your feet up?

I'm sure you can think of lots more examples yourself. The key thing is to have them written down and ready to hand, so they appear spontaneous.

Above all, never be sniffy about developing a personal touch with your customers, even if you know that you are unlikely ever to meet them in the flesh. Do not forget: business is all about people talking to people, not one set of functionaries talking to another set of functionaries. So get to know the person behind the voice, and try to make him feel good in the process. Write down which of your customers supports which football club, which of them likes painting, fishing, snooker, horse-riding, bridge or whatever. Remember (ie write down) which one has given up smoking and which one has a birthday on Christmas Day.

If you take an interest in your customers and if you make them feel good, you will find that they will do the same for you.

Adapting to the individual buyer

Assuming you have developed some sort of 'feel' for the individual at the other end of the phone, what then? How do you exploit this knowledge?

What you must do is to tailor your approach to fit in with that individual or with what that individual thinks is important.

Here are the *two most common buyer stereotypes* that you are likely to meet.

The first is a buyer who is particularly concerned with company procedure and formality. When dealing with this person, you must make quite sure that you stick to the procedures in question and avoid trying any shortcuts. You may have to send a formal letter, for example, explaining yourself, your company and your product. This may be in addition to your normal sales literature and samples. This formal communication may well be an essential prerequisite for such a buyer to consider speaking to you personally. You may even have to speak with one or more less senior members of the company (and gain their approval) before being allowed to speak to this type of buyer.

As you might have expected, our second stereotype is altogether different. This person is someone who seems almost to buy on impulse. He is very confident and prides himself on his ability to get to the heart of the matter, over the phone, without bothering with reams of paperwork. It goes without saying that the personal attitudes of this type of buyer have a much greater influence over what and how he buys than in our first example. As a result, getting to know this type of buyer will prove extremely worthwhile. However, despite his apparent informality, this type of buyer can be extremely difficult to handle. In particular, you must be fingertip ready with your facts and arguments and be well prepared to stand your ground or he will walk all over you.

Apart from these two common stereotypes of buyer, there are several other basic types and you really have to rely upon your own knowledge of people when it comes to dealing with them.

What I hope I have done is to alert you to the importance of the human element in selling over the phone. You must always remember that you are selling to a human being first and a buyer second and you must, therefore, adapt, your approach accordingly.

How to behave when a buyer 'grabs you by the throat'
Precisely because buyers are human beings, they can sometimes be ill-tempered and aggressive.

One of their most common reactions, when they are like this, is to grab you (metaphorically speaking) by the throat and accuse you of 'wasting their time'. They say things like, 'Not another bloody salesman! Why don't you push off and bother someone else?'

If this sort of thing happens then, for the sake of your own self-respect, if for no other reason, you should know how to behave and what to say. The general rule for how to react in such a situation is this:

Rule 4. Stay professional, stay cool and stay open for business

General approach
Whatever someone says to you, *never* lose your temper.

You must always remember that you are the representative of your company and its good name. Besides, abusing someone may cost you money. For example, the buyer who provokes you may have friends who are or who may be customers of yours. Both you and your product may suffer accordingly. Moreover, do not forget what I said earlier about buyers being under invisible pressure. Your nasty buyer may have received some bad news about something and may have simply blown his top in frustration. Usually, he may be perfectly reasonable.

In any event, by losing your temper you may find it very difficult to recontact the buyer and so you might lose a valuable source of business. So the message is this: whatever someone says to you, your general approach should be to stay professional, stay cool and stay open for business.

What to say
Assuming that you cannot defuse the situation by arranging to ring back at a more convenient time, here are four different things to say to your verbal assailant.

Buyers need salespeople
Tell him that buyers need salespeople to contact them. Without such contact, buyers would have to spend endless time and money ringing up dozens of different suppliers in an effort to find out what was available and what it cost.

To be efficient, buyers need advance information
You can also explain that even though buyers (like him) might not actually need a salesperson's product when he rings up, nevertheless the situation may change and such buyers would obviously benefit from already having the relevant information on file.

To be safe, buyers need alternative suppliers
You can also say that it usually pays buyers to buy products from more than one source. Tell him that, even if he already has a supplier for your type of product, he might still profit from giving you a share of his orders. (More competition and more reliability of supply.)

Buyers have salespeople too
Finally you can and should remind him that his company also employs salespeople who have to 'bother' potential customers. Ask him how what you are doing is any different from what his own salespeople are doing.

If you can put these points politely but firmly, to your assailant, you will go a long way towards calming him down, gaining his respect and maintaining your own personal integrity.

In the words of Eleanor Roosevelt: 'No one can make you feel inferior without your consent.'

Part Two
The Actual Sell

A special introduction

What you must do
In order to sell a product to a company over the telephone, you normally have to overcome five specific hurdles:

1. You must find out the name of the person to sell to (the buyer).
2. You must succeed in getting through to him.
3. You must canvass him.
4. You must present your product to him.
5. You must close him.

Although these hurdles have their own difficulties and complexities, they each present their own set of problems, so we shall, therefore, study each separately.

How you must think
In practice, telephone selling is about speaking to strangers who neither know you nor the product you are selling. In other words, both you and your product are going to be unfamiliar to your listener.

As a result, you must expect your listener to be uninterested and sceptical when you introduce yourself. You must expect him to be unconvinced by the benefits of your product when you introduce them to him. You must expect him to raise a dozen different objections when you ask him what he thinks and you must expect him to respond negatively when you ask him to buy.

In short, *you must expect people to disagree with you*, because only then will you be psychologically prepared for the patient and persistent phone-work which is necessary to overcome this disagreement and secure your sale.

6. How to Get the Buyer's Name and How to Get Through

For reasons that will soon become clear, these hurdles are best dealt with together: hence the reason for including both of them in the same chapter.

Before you can start selling something to a company over the phone, you need to know the name of the person who buys the sort of product you are offering and you have to get through to him. This is not always as straightforward as it sounds, because there are many other sales-people who are also trying to approach the same companies as you are. As a result, some companies become inundated with sales calls and so operate a 'screening' process to prevent certain callers from pestering their executives.

Examples

Salesperson: Could I speak to the person who buys your photocopying machines, please?

Receptionist: Just a moment. [Pause while she checks what to do with you] Hello? I'm sorry, I'm told we don't need any photocopiers at the moment. Goodbye.

Or:

Salesperson: Could I speak to the person who handles your advertising, please?

Receptionist: I'll just check who that is, just hold on a moment. [Pause, while she speaks to someone else for advice. As in the first example, she will know that you are a salesperson – in this case selling advertising – so she is checking to see whether to put you through to anybody.] Hello, I'm sorry, I'm told we're not doing any advertising at the moment. Can you ring back in a couple of months?

In both examples, our poor salesperson was fobbed off or screened before he even had a chance to give his name. To minimize the danger of this happening to you, you must understand this screening process: you must know how it works, what its weaknesses are and how they can be exploited.

The screening process

As you have just learned, a company operates a screening process to prevent its executives (directors, managers etc) from being pestered by too many calls. In simple terms, this process is operated by two different people: first, by the company receptionist, and secondly, by the executive's secretary.

Getting past reception

Usually, all you need to do in order to get past reception is to be able to quote the individual name of the person you wish to speak to, and then ask to be put through in a reasonably assured manner.

This may safely be achieved, using two calls or, less safely, with one.

Using two calls
One of the weaknesses of most screening processes is that they do not usually try to interfere with postal contact. This means that if you ask for the name of the relevant buyer in such a way as to suggest that you are only interested in contacting him by post, you will normally be given it without objection and you can then ring back later, suitably armed. For example:

Salesperson: Hello, I wonder if you can help me? I'd like to send some information to the person in charge of X (or buying X), but I don't have his name to hand. Who would that be, please?

Receptionist: Oh, that will be Mr Jones.

Salesperson: You wouldn't happen to know his first name, would you?

There are two things to note about this example. First, if the receptionist had put you on hold while she took advice on what to do with you, as in our earlier examples, she would have said that she had someone on the line who wanted the buyer's name in order to send him some information, not someone who wanted to speak to the buyer in question. In all probability, the name would have been given to her because you would not have been seen as a potential pest.

Secondly, by going one step further and asking for your contact's first name, you are preparing yourself even more thoroughly for when you ring back. After all, someone who asks to speak to Trevor Jones is usually assumed to know him better than someone who simply asks for Mr Jones.

OK, you now have a name. Now all that remains is to call back and demonstrate a reasonably assured manner when asking to be put through.

For example, do *not* say something like this:

'Hello, could I speak to Trevor Jones, please?'
'Hello, would it be possible to speak to Trevor Jones, please?'
'Hello, could I have a word with Trevor Jones, please?' or
'Hello, is Trevor Jones available, please?'

All these attempts lack authority and assurance. In effect, you are asking whether it is OK for you to be put through: you are asking for permission. Be more assertive and sound as if you know what you are doing. Say something like this:

'Hello, Trevor Jones, please.' or
'Hello, put me through to Trevor Jones will you, please.'

This sort of approach sounds more authoritative and you should find that it will get you past reception without any bother.

Using one call only

If you do not have the time to make two separate calls (one to get a name, another to get through), a certain amount of extra charm is required in order to get the name you want and to be put through, at the same time.

The problem you have to face is that, as we saw earlier, where a receptionist is under orders to screen unsolicited sales calls, she may put you on hold while she seeks advice about what to do with you. Then when she returns, as it were, she may present you with a blunt, 'No thanks', as in the following example:

Salesperson: I'd like to speak to the person in charge of buying your office furniture please. Could you tell me who that might be?

Receptionist: Who's calling please?

Salesperson: Mr Smith from Amazing Furniture Ltd.

Receptionist: Just one moment. [Asks for advice on what to do with you] Hello? I'm sorry, I'm told we're not interested at the moment.

See what I mean? Our salesperson lacked sufficient charm and paid the penalty. A better approach would be something like this:

Salesperson: Hello, I wonder if you can help me, please? I need to talk to the person who normally buys your office furniture. Unfortunately, I don't have his name to hand, you wouldn't happen to know who that might be, would you? *Or*

Salesperson: Hello, I wonder if you can help me, please? I need to talk to the person who normally buys your office furniture. I spoke to him not so long ago, but I seem to have mislaid his name. You wouldn't happen to know who this might be, would you? *Or*

Salesperson: Hello, I wonder if you could do me a big favour? I need to speak to the person who normally buys your office furniture. The only trouble is I seem to have mislaid his name. You wouldn't do me a big favour and tell me who this might be, would you?'

These are all variations on the same theme: be nice and ask for help. In addition, the odd tiny white lie about having spoken to the buyer before (preferably in the distant past) will not do any harm. Of course, it will not work with everyone, but do not forget: receptionists are human too! If you are nice and friendly to them, the chances are they will be nice to you.

Once the receptionist has given you the buyer's name, you should have less difficulty in being put through. Just say, 'Can you put me through, please?'

Getting past the secretary

This is more difficult. Busy directors and managers frequently employ a charming but extremely protective secretary to screen their incoming calls. Nevertheless, once again, by understanding her role and the way she works, you should not find her an insuperable obstacle.

The task of the secretary
One of the principal tasks of such a secretary is to ward off unnecessary

callers and thus allow the buyer to get on with his work, without unnecessary interruptions. Prime candidates for this sort of brush-off treatment include:

- callers who have been blacklisted by the buyer himself
- callers who are aggressive or impolite
- callers who are likely to take up a lot of the buyer's time
- callers who cannot explain clearly why they wish to be put through to the buyer.

The message must be: do not fall into any of these four categories. Do not, for example, allow yourself to become *persona non grata* with the buyer: do not be aggressive or impolite towards the secretary, and try to give her the strong impression that you only need a few moments of the buyer's time. Finally, make sure that you sound as though you know what you want. Hesitation or dithering can be fatal.

What to say
In addition to the above more general advice, you must also observe these specific rules:

- Sound assured. Do not ask for permission. Sound as though you know the buyer.
- Give out as little information as possible. That way there is less for the secretary to query.
- When pushed, sound polite, charming and appreciative of the secretary's help. Try to make an effort to smile when you are talking.
- Emphasize the speed and simplicity of your enquiry. Do not make it sound complicated or time-consuming.
- Above all, try to make it sound as though only the buyer can help you. Do not allow the secretary to feel that she can handle your enquiry herself: otherwise, she will.

With all this in mind, I will now give you a typical example of what to say in this type of situation and what you will typically encounter from a secretary.

Please note that in this, as in all other examples throughout the book, I am attempting to reproduce actual speech, which 'writes' differently from the way it 'sounds'. Try to make allowances for this as you read it. Finally, try to think up similar ways, yourself, of saying the things that I recommend. Think up your own examples: that way you will learn faster.

Example
Suppose you are canvassing a buyer from Sainsway Supermarkets. You have his name, but you have not spoken to him before. You manage to pass through reception and you are put through to the buyer's office.

Secretary: Hello, John Smith's office, can I help you?

Salesperson: Hello, is John Smith in, please?

Note: you can say this to a secretary but not to a receptionist. Note also that you are not asking permission to speak to John Smith or to be put through; you are simply asking if he is in and assuming that, if he is, you *will* be put through.

Secretary: Who's calling, please?

Salesperson: Susan Shaw.

Note: give out as little information as possible. The secretary might assume that you are a friend or acquaintance of John Smith or, at least, reasonably well known to him, and she might not, therefore, ask for any further identification before putting you through.

Secretary: From which company?

Note: It has not worked. She does not recognize your name and, therefore, asks for more details before deciding whether or not to put you through.

Salesperson: Overseas Fruit Limited.

Note: again, do not go into detail. She may put you straight through.

Secretary: Can I ask what it is concerning?

Note: this secretary is a tough cookie. Now you must demonstrate either that your call is necessary or, at the very least, that it will not inconvenience or delay the buyer.

Salesperson: Yes, of course. I need to speak to Mr Smith for a couple of minutes about the range of fruit we sell. Really, I just want to introduce myself and to ask him a couple of questions about the fruit he normally buys. Nothing more than that really, I'll only be a moment.

Note: You do not 'want' to speak to John Smith, you 'need' to. Note also the stress on 'speed' (eg, 'couple of minutes' and 'I'll only be a moment'). Also note the carefully expressed reason for calling: 'Really, I just want to introduce myself'. Finally, and most importantly, note the inclusion of the *vital* phrase, 'ask him a couple of questions about the fruit he normally buys'. This is said to deter the secretary from trying to handle the enquiry herself. She has to quickly ask herself, 'Can I explain the sort of fruit the company buys as well as my boss can?' Usually, the answer will be no and she might put you through.

Result
At this point, I think it would be likely that the secretary would speak to

her boss and then put you through. You appear to have satisfied most of her criteria and there appears to be very little for her to worry about. However, we shall assume that she does not connect you with the buyer, but, instead, falls back on a very common line.

Secretary: I'm very sorry. Mr Smith is busy just at the moment. Can I help you?

When a secretary says this, it can only mean one of two things: either the person is really busy or she is giving you the brush-off. Normally, if she says this to you on the first, or on the first couple of occasions when you call, you will have to take her word for it. However, if she persists with this line, you must assume that you are being fobbed off and you must react accordingly.

Where the buyer is genuinely busy
In this case, you should:

- Thank the secretary for her time and attention.
- Make whatever polite and charming small talk you can.
- Ask her to tell you when would be the most convenient time for you to call back. This is a key question, since her response will normally be a good indication of whether the buyer was genuinely busy or not. If she is reluctant to specify a time ('I'm afraid he's a very busy man', or, 'Well, it's difficult to say, he's in and out all the time'), you can take it for granted that you are being fobbed off.
- Tell her you will call back at the recommended time.

In other words, try to extricate yourself with a certain amount of charm. Do not make her feel unimportant by rushing to hang up.

Where you feel fairly certain you are being fobbed off
Your reaction in this case should vary with the circumstances. For example, if the company you are calling is potentially of great importance to you, you must perforce be a little more circumspect than if, say, the company is small and likely to be relatively unimportant.

To allow for both these types of situation, I will give you two examples of how to handle them: one soft and another slightly harder.

Soft reaction to being fobbed off

Secretary: [For the third or fourth time] I'm sorry, Mr Smith is busy just at the moment. Can I help you?

Salesperson: Well, yes, if you wouldn't mind. As I've explained, I'm trying to get through to have a quick word with Mr Smith [you can drop the John] about the sort of fruit he buys, and the sort of service he expects from suppliers and so on. The point is, we may have something which is of interest to him, but I need a brief word with him to check on a couple of details.

Note: this is all said slowly and clearly. You keep stressing 'need' to speak to the buyer and the fact you only need 'a quick word'. You also take care to state that you may have 'something which is of interest to him', but that you need to clarify a couple of things *with him* first. Again this is to prevent the secretary handling the matter herself.

Salesperson: Now obviously you know Mr Smith's workload better than anyone, so how do you suggest I proceed? How easy is it going to be to have a quick word with him?

Note: you end on a note of respect for the position of the secretary and ask an open question to find out whether she will help you.

At this point, the secretary will respond in one of two ways: she will either be helpful or unhelpful.

Helpful

Secretary: Well, as I've just said, Mr Smith is a very busy man. However, if it's really just a question of having a quick word with him, I suggest you try to catch him first thing in the morning.

Salesperson: Wonderful! When exactly?

Secretary: I should say just after 9 am. He's usually free for a few moments from 9.00 to 9.15.

Salesperson: I've made a note of that, that's perfect. Listen, thank you very much for your help, it's most appreciated. As you suggest, I'll call Mr Smith soon after 9.00 tomorrow.

Result
Since you appear to have won over the secretary, you should experience no further problem in getting through.

Unhelpful

Secretary: Well, I'm afraid, as I've said, Mr Smith is a very busy man, so I really can't say when he is likely to be free. Perhaps next week sometime.

In this situation, where the secretary is going out of her way to be unhelpful, but where her company is still potentially important to you, you have three options.

Option 1   Arrange to write a letter

Salesperson: Oh dear. This is an important matter and I do have to
make sure that Mr Smith knows about it. Perhaps I
should drop him a line and then have a word with him
afterwards. What do you think?

Note: you are not interested in her advice, as such. You are going to
write anyway, but you ask the question to probe for more information.
In any case, if she agrees with you, she is, in effect, agreeing to your
writing and then speaking to the buyer afterwards. Something you may
remind her of, on a future occasion.

Result
She is almost certain to agree that you should write a letter. This letter
may be followed up in due course and will usually provide you with the
excuse to be put through. It just takes time.

Option 2   Arrange to speak to someone else in the company

Salesperson: Oh dear. This is an important matter. Tell me, who else
in the company handles fruit buying for you?

Note: you are putting pressure on the secretary to provide you with
another contact with whom you can discuss this 'important matter'. It is
always possible that if she cannot give you another name, she might put
you through. At the very least, you are demonstrating that you are not
going to go quietly: you intend to pursue your 'important matter'.

Result
If she does give you the name of another person to contact, he is more
likely to be a junior employee and not someone with real authority.
However, at least you will be able to get through to him and you must
try to discover from him as much information as possible about the
original buyer (especially, for example, how to get past his secretary).
You should be able to do this reasonably easily; it just takes time.

Option 3   You can press on
Note: ideally you have found out the secretary's name from reception
during one of your earlier calls. You might even have discovered
something about her from another member of staff (eg she plays a lot of
tennis, she has been with the company for 30 years, she has just returned
from a fortnight's holiday in Greece) which might give you an 'edge'
when it comes to establishing rapport.

Salesperson: Look, Mrs X, I don't wish to be a nuisance. I mean I
realize that both you and Mr Smith are very busy people,

but so am I. Now you must know Mr Smith's workload inside out; there has to be a tiny space in it for me to have a quick word with him. I wouldn't be pushing like this if the matter wasn't important, but it is. So is there any chance of you fitting me in for a quick word on the phone sometime?

Note: this is the furthest you can go and still be 'soft'. Remember to speak slowly and clearly and *smile* down the phone.

Result

If the secretary appreciates your sincerity and seriousness, she will probably arrange for you to ring back and speak to Mr Smith. If she does not, and simply repeats the fact that he is a busy man, you may either choose to use Options 1 or 2, or you can decide to ring the secretary back again and again. And in case this last idea sounds too much like knocking your head against the proverbial brick wall, I can tell you from personal experience that nothing succeeds quite like perseverance.

Slightly harder reaction to being fobbed off

Secretary: [For the third or fourth time] I'm sorry, Mr Smith is busy just at the moment. Can I help you?

Salesperson: Oh dear, I appear to be permanently out of luck, this is the third or fourth time I've called. What do I have to do to get you to put me through, sing you a song?! [Or choose something else which you consider more suitable.]

Secretary: [Refusing to be swayed] I'm sorry, there's really nothing I can do.

Salesperson: Well, I wish my secretary was as efficient as you. I only hope they are paying you enough! Look, I realize that you've got a job to do, but so have I. I don't want to speak to Mr Smith in order to try and sell him something [a white lie]. All I want to do is to have a quick word with him, ask him a couple of questions and arrange to send him a quotation/brochure/information pack. I'll only be a moment. Now I'm sure you can squeeze me into Mr Smith's timetable somewhere, so when can I grab a moment with him?

Result

If the secretary recognizes your sincerity and seriousness, in all probability she will arrange a time for you to call back and speak to Mr

Smith. If she does not, then, in practice, considering the value of the company to you, you are wasting your time and money attempting to make contact on the phone. You may, however, decide to persevere by post.

Conclusion

Try not to be alarmed by the idea of being screened by receptionists and secretaries. It is a very standard company practice and usually operates in a perfectly reasonable manner. Besides, your company will almost certainly screen its own incoming calls, so you cannot really complain.

The important thing is to be aware of what to expect and that you have to work at getting a name and then work at being put through to the buyer. Once you know what to expect, you will be suitably prepared. With luck, if you have read this chapter carefully and if you are willing to practise the things you have learned, you will be capable of handling even the toughest screening procedures.

7. How to Canvass Your Buyer

So you have found out the name of the buyer and you are put through –
now what? How do you go about introducing yourself, your company
and your product to this stranger?

Answer: you use the *150-second canvassing call method*.

This is an excellent scheme to follow when contacting a buyer for the
first time. It's easy to remember, it's practical and, above all, it's flexible.
If you encounter any difficulties from the buyer, you can usually switch
from one section of the call to another, without losing your flow.

It is called the *150-second canvassing call method* for the simple
reason that 150 seconds is about the maximum time you can expect to
be allowed from a buyer who knows nothing about you. Indeed, both
the total time of the call (150 seconds) and the times of the call's com-
ponent sections (discussed below) are only given as guidelines. They are
there to remind you to push on and not to waste time.

Having said all this, I do not want you to feel that simply memorizing
the method itself will be sufficient. You must certainly study it carefully
but you should also spend time practising it and adapting it, where
necessary, to your own particular product and your own individual
style.

This is your most important sales call

The basic telephone sales method outlined in this book consists of three
different calls: first, a call to introduce yourself and to arrange to send
information about your product (the canvassing call); second, a call to
present the benefits of your product (the presentation call); and third, a
call to finalize the deal (the closing call).

Clearly, unless you are successful with your canvassing call, you are
not going to be given a chance to make any further calls to the company

in question. You must, therefore, practise your canvassing call until you are word-perfect and ready to cope with just about anyone or anything. It is the first and most important call of the entire sales process.

Making appointments
Many tele-sales staff specialize in making appointments only. They telephone companies across the country, arranging appointments with buyers for travelling sales representatives. The 150-second canvassing call method is also an ideal and easily adaptable method for making such appointments.

An outline of the 150-second canvassing call method

The call is divided into the following sections:

- The 30-second 'first impression'
- The 30-second 'link'
- The 60-second 'quiz'
- The 30-second 'close'

The 30-second 'first impression'

This is the most important part of the call: as the saying goes, 'You never get a second chance to make a first impression'. If you begin well, the rest of the call should be relatively easy. On the other hand, if you start sloppily, it will probably be uphill all the way.

What you must do
In the first 30 seconds, you must explain who you are, where you are calling from, what your company does and, if necessary, which specific product you are selling. If you prefer, you may end on a neutral question.

How to speak
As explained in Chapter 4, you should take the greatest possible care to allow your listener to 'wake up' and adjust to your 'alien' voice. Thus, you must speak slowly and clearly and avoid using any complex terminology that might not be immediately understood. Keep it slow, keep it simple and keep it understandable.

Here are some examples of what to say:

Example No 1
You are selling stationery products to companies. Your name is Sarah Brown, your work for Easiprint Ltd. You are telephoning a company for the first time. The buyer's name is Mr Smith.

Salesperson: Hello, Mr Smith. I don't think that we have spoken together before. My name is Sarah Brown. I work for Easiprint Ltd. We supply a range of stationery items to several hundred companies throughout the London area: everything from typing and computer paper to adding machines and staplers. Not the most exciting stuff in the world, I'm afraid, but it keeps offices running nice and smoothly ... [pause to allow the buyer to interject.]

Note how you deliberately extend your initial phrases. This is to allow your listener to adjust and gradually 'wake up' to what is going on. Nothing is more irritating for a buyer than to have a salesperson ring up and start gabbling away before he is able to catch on to what is being said. You avoid this mistake.

Note also the simple and informative language used to paint an instant picture of what you do. It is reinforced by the careful reference to the 'several hundred' customers who already buy from you. This should inspire confidence in your company.

Note also your final, down-to-earth comment which associates your company with smooth-running offices. Apart from being the number one benefit of your product, this should also relax your listener by introducing a lighter note to the conversation.

Example No 2
You are selling a range of fresh coffees to hotels and restaurants. You work for Café Deluxe Ltd. Your name is Frank James. You are telephoning a hotel for the first time. The buyer's name is Mr Jones.

Salesperson: Mr Jones. I don't think that we have spoken together before. My name is Frank James. I work for Café Deluxe Ltd, based in London. We supply a wide range of luxury coffees, Parisian continental coffees, that sort of thing – the type of coffee you used to be able to buy in those specialized luxury coffee houses. I'm sure you know what I mean. You're not a coffee enthusiast yourself by any chance, are you? [pause.]

Note that here you are selling a much more specialized product. Hence a little more definition is required. Having said that, words like 'continental' are put in more to give the listener's ear something to remember than to accurately describe the product. Note also the use of the phrase 'specialized luxury coffee houses', both to paint a picture of the product and to associate it with the idea of luxury, quality and expense.

Note how you end with a deliberately innocuous question. It really does not matter whether the buyer is a coffee drinker or not: the point is you are drawing him into the conversation in a light-hearted and relaxing way.

The pause

As you can see, at the end of your introduction, you pause to allow the buyer to interject if he so wishes. Occasionally, (or when you first start selling), you may feel more comfortable by asking a fairly simple question in order to give your listener something specific to respond to. In the coffee example, I have listed one such question, although there are others. For example, you can end by saying, 'Does that make sense?', or 'Am I making sense?', or 'Are you with me, so far?'

These are all questions which really have to be answered affirmatively, so you need not worry that you are giving the other person a chance to say 'No'. However, it is not strictly necessary to end with a question, more a matter of individual taste, so do as you prefer.

The buyer's reaction to your pause

Whether you end your introduction with a question or not, the buyer will react to your pause in one of three ways.

He may indicate that you should continue. Either he will answer your innocuous question with something like, 'No, as a matter of fact I hate coffee...', or he will grunt or otherwise indicate that you should continue. In either case, you should pass on to the next section of the call, the '30-second link' (see below).

He may say he is busy and ask you to call back. In this case, get him to suggest a convenient time for you to ring back. Remember to note it down and call back as arranged. You should then begin the canvassing call all over again.

He may say, 'Not interested'. *Do not be in the least bit put off by this.* Most people who say, 'Not interested' do so out of laziness or inconvenience. Understand this reaction and try not to be put off.

What you must do is to ask him very politely why he is saying 'No' to something that has not as yet been explained to him. This will normally provoke one of two replies.

First, he may confess that he really cannot be bothered to listen to what you have to say. He is far too busy at the moment. If this is really his objection, you should try to arrange a call back, as above.

Secondly, he may say something like, 'I don't want any more stationery/coffee. I've already got quite enough, thank you'. Here you should use a technique called 'Hold on tight and answer back'.

The hold on tight and answer back technique

What the buyer wants to do is to get rid of you, so do not let him; *hold on tight* instead. The best way to do this is to ask him two or three open questions, which you have carefully prepared beforehand.

For example, if you are selling fax machines you might ask, 'Oh, what sort of machines do you have, Mr Smith?', followed by 'And how long have you had them?', and, 'Do you lease them or have you bought them outright?' and so on.

Ask him anything that will keep him talking and allow you time to put your thoughts in order, but which also might give you a glimpse of what lies behind his apparent lack of interest.

After asking him these questions and perhaps regaining some of the initiative, you should then very politely but firmly *answer back*. For example, you should try to put across the following argument:

● Listening to you and to what you have to say will cost him nothing.
● On the contrary, he may actually be impressed.
● If he is, he will know where to buy his fax machines or any other products the next time he needs them.
● Tell him (if it's true) that you have lots of customers who did not buy from you to start with because, like him, they already stocked other products. However, they *listened* to what you had to say, they were impressed and now they buy from you. Ideally, quote numbers of customers or actual customers' names.
● Suggest, therefore, that you ring back when it's more convenient for him.

Above all, when it comes to challenging someone who says, 'Not interested', be very polite and charming but also be persistent. If you can manage to do all this, you will definitely get a reasonable number of these listeners to think again.

Read over this section again very carefully. Try to prepare a specific script for what to say if you have someone on the phone who reacts in this way. You will find it invaluable until you learn how to handle yourself properly. It is yet another one of those examples where preparation plus practice make perfect.

The 30-second 'link'

As the name suggests, this section acts as a link between your 'first impression' and your 'quiz'. The key thing about this section is to try and steer your buyer directly into the 'quiz' *without giving him an opportunity of interjecting any further*.

What you must do

● Stress that you are really just calling to introduce yourself.
● Say that you do not wish to go into detail about your product just at the moment.
● Tell the buyer that what you would like to do is to ask him a little more about his business, for example ... (do not pause).

How to speak

Because, by this stage of the call, your listener will be fully alert, you can speed up your delivery. Even so, you should still make an effort to speak clearly and avoid jargon. I recommend that you concentrate on being fluent and articulate.

Here are some examples of what to say:

Example No 1 (continued from p 64)

Salesperson: The reason I'm ringing is really just to introduce myself. I don't want to go into chapter and verse about how good our stationery service is or why people buy from us, just at the moment – I think it's probably a bit soon for that. What I *would* like to do, if you can spare me half a minute, is to ask you exactly what your company does. For example, I have you down as an electrical wholesaler. Is that correct?

Note that you immediately relax the buyer by telling him that you are really calling to introduce yourself, rather than to try and sell him something. Of course, this is a white lie. Should the opportunity arise, you will try to sell him as much as you can, but the important thing is that he feels relaxed and able to listen to (and, if necessary, discuss) what you have to say.

Note also how you are asserting yourself. In particular, phrases like, 'I don't want to...', and, 'What I would like to do is...' give the impression of someone in control of himself and what he wants to achieve.

Finally, note how you move from telling him what you *would* like to do (ask him questions) to actually doing it. In most cases, the buyer will simply go on to answer your questions without objection.

Example No 2 (continued from p 64)

Salesperson: Actually, the reason I'm ringing, Mr Jones, is really just to introduce myself. I don't want to go into great detail about how good our coffees are or how you can make money out of us; it's too soon for that. What I would like to do, if you've got a moment, is to ask you about your hotel. For example, I've got it down as a three-star hotel with 40 bedrooms: is that right? You haven't had a bowling alley or an indoor swimming pool added recently, have you?'

Note a very similar approach to that of our first example. You end with a similar sort of question – with a humorous twist in this case – which the buyer can hardly fail to respond to.

In both cases, you will probably find that the buyer will answer your question without objection. If he does, you have automatically entered the third section of your call – the 'quiz' section – and you may proceed by asking further questions (as set out below). If, by chance, the buyer objects to answering your question and says, 'Not interested', you must query his lack of interest in the way that I outlined on p 65 in the 'hold on tight and answer back' section.

Is it necessary to check that your buyer has authority?
Some sales methods recommend that you specifically ask your listener to confirm that he has authority to buy, early in the call. I do not agree with this; at least, I do not recommend it for anyone who is new to selling. And for three reasons.

First, because, in practice, your listener will usually interrupt and tell you if he is not the person with authority. Secondly, because asking leading questions early in the call can disrupt your flow. After all, asking someone if he *can* buy something sounds suspiciously like asking him if he *will* buy that something – at least it does to buyers! Thirdly, given that you have already checked at reception, and possibly with his secretary, that your listener is the relevant buyer, there appears to be little to be gained from reopening the issue at this stage.

What you have achieved so far
You have introduced yourself and painted a quick picture of what you do. You have relaxed your listener by telling him that, instead of trying to sell him something straightaway, you would like to talk about his business. Above all, you have probably been on the phone for over a minute and your presentation is still 'intact'. In this connection, it is worth noting that, not only do most sales attempts fail inside the first minute, but the longer you are on the phone, the greater the rapport between yourself and your listener and the greater your chance of making a sale.

The 60-second 'quiz'

In my experience, too many salespeople undervalue the importance of asking the buyer what his company does and how it does it.

In fact, this question and answer routine not only allows you to pinpoint the *needs* of the buyer's company (which is vital when it comes to matching them with the appropriate benefits of your product), it also helps you to deal with any objections the buyer himself makes later in the call. Finally, by showing an interest in what the buyer's own company does (indeed, by simply prolonging the call), it helps you to further your telephone rapport with your listener, with obviously beneficial results.

So take note and make this quiz an important part of your call.

What to do
Obviously, the type of questions you ask will vary with the type of products you are selling and the type of customer you are selling to. Nevertheless, the aim is to discover some or all of the following:

● General information about what the company does and how it does it (ie, how much of your product might the company need to buy in order to run its business efficiently). This will enable you to form an opinion as to how valuable a customer the company might be.
● More specific information about the type of competitive products currently used by the company. Among other things, this will show you what you are up against.
● Any information about what the buyer himself thinks about the company, its business and the product you are selling. As explained in Chapter 5, knowing what your buyer thinks about something will help you to adjust your approach accordingly.

How to speak
Do not make the buyer feel that you are in any way prying or asking for confidential information. Steer clear of asking for particularly detailed information. Try to go from the general to the specific. Listen carefully and stay alert.

Here are some examples of what to say:

Example No 1 (continued from p 67)
Assuming that the buyer confirms that he is working for an electrical wholesaler, the salesperson should proceed directly into the quiz section by asking the following types of question; the buyer's answers are given in shorthand form, in brackets.

Salesperson: And what sort of electrical products do you specialize in?

Buyer: (All types: cookers, ovens, washing machines, tumble dryers, fridges, heaters, vacuum cleaners.)

Salesperson: And whom do you sell to, in the main?

Buyer: (Mostly shops, but also to individuals at a public counter.)

Salesperson: How are you finding business overall?

Buyer: (Getting better.)

Salesperson: What about repairs? How much are you involved in repairs?

Buyer: (Repairs are a large part of the business.)

Salesperson: Roughly how many office or administration staff do you have?

Buyer:	(About ten.)
Salesperson:	To what extent are you computerized?
Buyer:	(All stock and all accounts are fully computerized.)
Salesperson:	And how do you get your stationery at the moment?
Buyer:	(From one local distributor.)
Salesperson:	How often do you usually order?
Buyer:	(About once a fortnight.)
Salesperson:	Finally, can I ask you what you look for in a stationery supplier?
Buyer:	(Fast, reliable service.)

Note how you moved from the general to the specific and how you end on a slightly more personal note. Note that you avoid confidential questions like, 'What is your turnover?', or 'Where does your profit come from?' Obviously, it is too soon for this sort of question.

Note how nearly all your questions are open questions. You therefore make it difficult for the buyer to avoid giving you information.

Note how nearly all your questions relate to your product. For example, the different products that the company sells and the different types of customers sold to, will determine the amount of paperwork generated. Each shop customer, for example, will require a delivery note, an invoice, a statement of account, plus one or two reminders – all of which probably have to be produced in triplicate. Furthermore, items sold that are then returned for repair attract additional paperwork, again in triplicate. The number of office staff can also give you a guide as to the amount of stationery items consumed.

Note, finally, how you find out where the buyer gets his stationery from and what he looks for in a supplier. You have learned, for example, that your competitor is probably a small company and that your buyer is not necessarily cost-conscious. Just these two pieces of knowledge alone will help you greatly when it comes to presenting your product. All in all, this is a potentially valuable customer.

Example No 2 (continued from p 67)
Assuming that the buyer confirms that the hotel has 40 bedrooms and three stars, the salesperson should proceed directly into the quiz section of the call by asking the following types of question.

Salesperson:	When is your busiest time?
Buyer:	(Generally, weekdays and the main holidays, Christmas and Easter.)

Salesperson:	How many holidaymakers do you get?
Buyer:	(Not many; business is mainly commercial travellers.)
Salesperson:	What meals do you normally serve?
Buyer	(Usually just dinner and breakfast; no lunches.)
Salesperson:	What about business functions? How many of these do you do?
Buyer:	(No business functions, there are no facilities.)
Salesperson:	Do you serve morning or afternoon coffee?
Buyer:	(Yes, both.)
Salesperson:	How popular is this? How much business does this bring you?
Buyer:	(Quite a lot.)
Salesperson:	Where would this normally be served? Would it be in your general reception area or do you have a special lounge?
Buyer:	(In a separate, fairly spacious lounge.)
Salesperson:	What about the coffee you serve: Do you order it specially or do you use your normal catering supplier?
Buyer:	(The buyer buys a normal 'instant' coffee from the local cash-and-carry.)
Salesperson:	What do you look for in a supplier? What's important to you?
Buyer:	(Reliability. Things arriving on time.)
Salesperson:	As a matter of interest, how long have you been with the hotel?
Buyer:	(Eight years. The buyer owns it.)

Note, once again, how your questions are so phrased to find out how easy it is for the hotel to make use of your product.

So, for example, the type of guest the hotel receives, the meals that are served and the staging of business functions (or not) are all useful indicators of whether and to what extent the hotel may buy your coffee. Unfortunately, from what you are told, the hotel will probably have less use for your coffee than is usual under the circumstances. For example, it has few holidaymakers (who have both the time and the money to indulge themselves), it does not serve lunch (one less meal to serve your coffee with) and it has no business functions (no opportunity to impress companies with the quality of the coffee). Fortunately, though, you have found out that the hotel does run a reasonably successful morning and afternoon coffee service: this should give it at least two regular opportunities to make use of your coffee.

Note, also, that asking where the morning and afternoon coffee service is provided has given you a further clue as to the potential of this service. The fact that a large separate lounge is used is an indicator of the importance of the service.

As in the first example, note that you discover who your competitor is, what the buyer himself looks for in a supplier and how you end on a personal note.

Overall, it sounds as if the hotel is a potentially 'modest' customer.

What you have achieved so far

With the completion of your quiz, you should now be in possession of enough information to know how valuable your customer might be, what product or service you have to compete against and, lastly, what attitude the buyer has towards new suppliers. If you have managed to learn all this, then your quiz has worked well.

You must now proceed to the final segment of your canvassing call – the close.

The 30-second close

This is the final part of the call, the moment when you close down the present conversation and set up conditions for a new one. You must take care to stay in control of the conversation until the very end.

What you must do

- Thank the buyer for his time and attention, and the information he has given you.
- Arrange to send him your product brochure and/or samples.
- Arrange to ring him back at a specific and convenient time in order to discuss the matter further.

How to speak

You must sound calm and self-assured right up to the time you say goodbye and hang up. Try to resist the natural temptation to speed up (and thereby lose your poise) as the end approaches.

Here are some examples of what to say:

Example No 1 (continued from p 70)

Salesperson: Listen, Mr Smith, thanks very much indeed for your time and trouble. The information you've given me will be a great help. What I'll do now is to send you our special information pack on the stationery service we provide, so you can see for yourself exactly what we offer. I'll leave it with you for a couple of days and give you a ring, say, Friday and we can then discuss the matter in a little more detail. How's that?

Buyer: OK.

Salesperson: When's the best time to get hold of you?

Buyer: Oh, make it the morning.

Salesperson: About 9.30?

Buyer: Yes, that's fine.

Salesperson: Right, I'll call you Friday at 9.30. Thanks very much, Mr Smith.

Note how you describe your information pack as 'special'. Try to use this word whenever possible. Note also the use of the open question 'How's that?' when you confirm your call back. As mentioned earlier, in Chapter 4, by asking an open question in such a case, you effectively force the buyer to suggest an alternative time if the suggested one is inconvenient. Note, finally, how you persist until the very end in establishing a specific time to call back. This is definitely worth the effort.

Example No 2 (continued from p 71)

Salesperson: Look, Mr Jones, thanks very much indeed for your time and trouble. The information you've given me will be a great help. Personally, I find that, if I know something about the business of the person I'm talking to, I can usually be of greater assistance. Anyway, what I'll do is to send you our special information pack on the coffees we provide and the back-up service that goes with them. I'll leave it with you then for a couple of days and I'll give you a call, say, Friday. How's that?

Buyer: I'm out Friday, better make it Thursday.

Salesperson: When's the best time, how about 2.00?

Buyer: No, leave it a little later, make it about 3.00.

Salesperson: Right, I'll be back to you Thursday at 3.00. Thanks very much.

Note, apart from the insertion of the phrase that you can be 'of greater assistance' now that he has given you some information about the hotel (a nice touch), the rest is almost identical to the first example.

8. How to Present Your Product to Your Buyer

An outline of the problems involved

We now come to the presentation call – the moment when you present your product to your buyer. Of all your calls, this is probably the most complicated and, therefore, the most demanding.

- To begin with you must reintroduce yourself and quickly renew the telephone rapport, which, you hope, you established with your canvassing call.
- Next, you must convince your still unenthusiastic listener that he will benefit by listening to an explanation of what your product will do for him. This is essential, because, unless you can first secure his co-operation in this way, any attempt on your part to explain your product will be met with a combination of disagreement and interruption.
- Having got your buyer to listen (albeit temporarily), you should immediately proceed to present your product. You should be brief, as well as interesting, but, above all, you must demonstrate that your product is what the buyer 'needs'.

Throughout this explanation section, you will probably be asked a variety of questions, some of which will bring you to a temporary halt before the buyer is sufficiently satisfied with your answers and allows you to proceed.

- Finally, after all this, you must bring matters to a close by suggesting that the buyer buys the product. This suggestion is usually greeted by the standard (and highly ambiguous) reply, 'I'll have to think about it'. Your reaction here should be to probe a little further to discover what your buyer means by this comment and then to arrange a call back as soon as possible.

So, as you can see, you have a lot to do and probably not a lot of time to do it in. The pressure will, therefore, be on you right from the start, to keep the conversation moving in the right direction and to keep your listener interested and attentive.

How to get the most out of this chapter

I have deliberately started this chapter with an account of the problems involved in making a presentation call, not to depress you – there are answers to most if not all of these problems – but to show you the amount of work which must be done if you want to master this type of call.

So, for example, apart from studying the basic presentation call method which is outlined in this chapter and 'speaking through' the practical examples given, you should also try drawing up your own product scripts and role-playing them with a friend or colleague.

I cannot over-emphasize the fact that the more you can practise presenting a product before picking up the phone for real, the better prepared you will be and the better you will sound.

Making your presentation call

You have canvassed your buyer and you have sent him the special information pack on your products. You now call him back as arranged. What do you say? How do you go about presenting your product to this unenthusiastic listener?

Answer: you use the *'four-part presentation call method'*.

This method, like the canvassing method we discussed in the last chapter, is both practical and flexible.

It is practical, because it teaches you how to deal with things in a simple, logical sequence which will help to protect you against customer interruption and objection.

It is flexible, because, if a customer does try to speed you up or interrupt you, you can usually switch from one part of the call to another, without losing your flow.

I recommend that you study this method carefully and then adapt it to your own particular products and to your own individual style.

The 'four-part presentation call'

As the name suggests, the call is divided into four parts as follows:

● The 'go back over' section

- The 'need' section (plus the 'if-question')
- The 'presentation' section
- The 'suggestion' section.

The 'go back over' section

What you must do
You must reintroduce yourself, you must check that your product information has arrived, and then you must tell the buyer that you would like to *go back over* what he told you last time about his company.

How to speak
Throughout the whole of this call, your tone must be confident and firm. Apart from taking the usual precautions to speak slowly, clearly and simply, you must make an effort to sound positive and businesslike. Do not forget you have to convince your buyer, during this call, that you have the answer to his needs or problems. So sound as though you are in control and that you know what you are talking about.

Here are some examples of what to say:

Example No 1 (continued from p 73)

Salesperson:	Hello, Mr Smith. If you recall, we spoke together at the beginning of the week about the stationery service we provide for companies in the London area. It's Sarah Brown here, from Easiprint.
Buyer:	Oh, yes.
Salesperson:	Now, since we spoke, you should have received the special information pack I sent you, which explains all about us. Do you remember getting it?
Buyer:	Vaguely, yes.
Salesperson:	Good, I'll come to that in a moment. First, if possible, I'd like to go back over a couple of things you told me last time about how your company works and so on. For example, I think you said that both your stock and your accounts are fully computerized. Is that right?

Note that your opening introduction is shorter here than at the beginning of your canvassing call. You are, therefore, giving your listener less time to 'wake up'. Try to compensate by making sure you say these words as slowly as possible. After your introduction, note how you confirm the arrival of your information pack. You do not ask whether the buyer has 'seen' it (which is quite irrelevant) but whether he has 'got' it. This is to stop the buyer from cutting short the conversation because he has not yet had a chance to read the relevant information. In my experience, buyers never admit to having read information sent to them by salespeople, even if (which is usually the case) they have quickly glanced at it.

Notice the unenthusiastic reaction by the buyer to your call and how you deal with it: you either ignore it, or you turn it into something more positive. Your expression, 'Good, I'll come to that in a moment', is a perfect example of how to sound positive in the face of such lack of interest. The key thing to note, however, about this opening section is how you avoid giving your buyer the opportunity to object to your call and how you steer him directly into the next part of the call. Provided you do not try to rush your final question, you will find that most buyers will answer without objection and allow you to continue with the next part of your call.

Example No 2 (continued from p 73)

Salesperson: Hello, Mr Jones. If you recall, we spoke together at the beginning of the week about our luxury coffee. It's Frank James here from Café Deluxe Limited.

Buyer: Oh, yes, I remember.

Salesperson: Now, in the meantime, you should have received our special information pack which I sent you. I don't know whether you remember getting it? It tells you about all the awards our coffees have won and so on.

Buyer: Yes, I think it arrived yesterday.

Salesperson: Good, I'll come back to that in a moment or two. First, I'd just like to go back over what you told me last time about the hotel. For example, I think you said that most of your guests are commercial people as opposed to tourists or other holidaymakers?

A very similar approach to our first example. You stay in control of the conversation and steer the buyer directly into the following 'quiz' section.

The 'need' section (plus the 'if-question')

What you must do

This is probably the most difficult section of the whole call. Put simply, *you must persuade the buyer to allow you to tell him about your product.* Unfortunately, you will find many buyers will object to this and will resist your suggestion that they listen for a moment to what you have to say. I suggest, therefore, that you tackle things in the following sequence:

● You must ask a few carefully prepared questions designed to find out more about the specific needs, or, rather, the specific *need*, of the buyer.
● After listening to what the buyer has to say, you must be able to sum up *this need* in a single sentence which you then repeat back to him for confirmation.

Note that when summing up the buyer's 'need' in this way, it is usually best to focus on one important need, or one important problem which he has to solve.

● Once the buyer has confirmed this need, you must ask the all-important 'if-question' – ie, 'If I can show you a way of satisfying this basic need, I presume that you'll give it a try?'

Example No 1 (continued from p 76)
Assume that the buyer confirms that both his stock and accounts are fully computerized.

Salesperson: And I presume, therefore, that most of your basic paperwork – delivery notes, invoices, statements and so on – is printed by the computer itself, none of it is pre-printed?

Buyer: That's right.

Salesperson: You must be getting through a fair amount of computer paper then?

Buyer: 'Fraid so.

Salesperson: What other stationery do you get through, in quantity?

Buyer: Oh, envelopes, typing paper, a few computer files, pens, that sort of thing.

Salesperson: Typewriter ribbons?

Buyer: Oh, yes.

Salesperson: Can you think of anything else? I mean things that you order regularly.

Buyer: Not really.

Salesperson: OK, now you said last time that – at the moment – you buy all your stationery from one local supplier. Is that right?

Buyer:	Yes, we just use the one.
Salesperson:	What's his catalogue like: does he carry most of the stuff you need?
Buyer:	Yes, most of it.
Salesperson:	And anything he hasn't got, I presume, he can order for you?
Buyer:	Yes, that's right.
Salesperson:	OK, now what about ordering? I think you told me that you usually order fortnightly?
Buyer:	Usually, yes.
Salesperson:	And you can get away with that, I presume, because most of your business is fairly regular – you don't have any sudden mad rushes or anything like that?
Buyer:	Not usually, no.
Salesperson:	So you don't usually need your stationery delivered overnight?
Buyer:	No.
Salesperson:	But what you do need, I presume, is a supplier who is *reliable* – in other words, someone who can guarantee to get you what you want and who can get it for you at a good price, would that be right?
Buyer:	I wouldn't disagree with that.
Salesperson:	So, if I can demonstrate a better service and lower prices than you are getting at the moment, then really you'd be a fool not to give us a try, wouldn't you?
Buyer:	Well, I might think about it.

Note the point behind these questions. First of all, you check that the customer has no unusual needs, no peculiar items of stationery that he uses regularly. Secondly, you check on your competitor – the buyer's current supplier. In this connection, note the carefully phrased question, 'Does he carry *most* of the stuff you need?' You do not give your buyer the opportunity of expressing total satisfaction in his supplier by asking, 'Does he carry *all* of the stuff you need?' That would be tantamount to inviting disaster if the buyer were to respond 'Yes'. Anyway, you find out that sometimes the supplier is unable to supply the buyer with certain items (because he does not carry them in stock) and, therefore, has to order them specially. This cannot be to the buyer's satisfaction.

Note, finally, how you sum up the buyer's basic need for 'reliability' in such a way that he really has no option but to agree with you. He may not sound very enthusiastic about it – buyers rarely do – but at least you have got him to concede that what you have to offer might be to his advantage, and, therefore, worth listening to. You can now proceed directly to present (ie, explain) your product.

One final point is the general level of interest expressed by your listener. It is really quite low. Unfortunately, you will encounter this time and time again when you sell over the phone. Most buyers talk to so many salespeople, about so many products, that they find it difficult to respond to yet another product, with any enthusiasm.

Example No 2 (continued from p 77)
Assume that the buyer confirms that his guests are mainly commercial people.

Salesperson:	And I presume this means that most of them are out all day and just come in towards evening, for their dinner and then breakfast the following morning?
Buyer:	Yes, that's about it.
Salesperson:	But, in addition to these residents, you also have a reasonable amount of passing trade in the way of morning and afternoon teas and coffees, don't you?
Buyer:	Yes, that's right.
Salesperson:	And most of this is served in your lounge?
Buyer:	Yes, that's right.
Salesperson:	OK, there's just one more thing, Mr Jones. I don't think I asked you this last time: how much do you actually charge for your coffee, say if someone comes in and orders afternoon coffee for example?
Buyer:	Oh, about a pound.
Salesperson:	And with breakfast or dinner, how much is it then?
Buyer:	About 70 pence.
Salesperson:	OK, I've got that. Well, Mr Jones, from what you've told me, you've got the customers and you've got the facilities. Your only problem – I suppose like most hoteliers – is getting your customers to part with their money? Would that be fair?

Buyer:	I suppose so.
Salesperson:	So would I be right in assuming that *if* I could show you a way of getting these customers to spend more money with you, you'd give it a try?
Buyer:	You mean by selling them your coffee?
Salesperson:	Exactly.
Buyer:	Maybe.

Note that you ask fewer questions in this example, because you have no real competitor to find out about. Instead, you focus on when exactly the hotel serves its coffee (mealtimes plus mornings and afternoons) and how much it charges. This last piece of information will be important later on in the call.

Note how you then move to defining the buyer's basic need – in this case, you express it in the form of a *problem* to be overcome – and how you phrase your 'if-question'. Once again, the buyer doesn't exactly sound over the moon about things, but at least he concedes that listening to you *might* help him. This is sufficient for you to proceed with your presentation.

A word of reassurance for all beginners

Please do not be put off or intimidated by the apparent complexity of this 'need' section: in practice, it is really much simpler than it sounds. The important thing is to try and get a *feel* for what you have to do.

In essence, you must get the buyer to talk to you about his business. Then, you simply put it to him that what he really needs is 'X', or that his basic problem is 'X'. Finally, after he has agreed that he really needs 'X', you say to him – as nicely as you can – 'So *if* I can show you that, by buying my product, you will in effect be getting 'X', then I presume you'll give it a try?' – or words to that effect.

It is quite a simple routine really: all it needs is a bit of practice. Try role-playing it with a friend. After a quarter of an hour or so, you will probably find that the whole thing becomes quite natural.

The 'presentation' section

This is the moment you have been working and waiting for: the opportunity to finally say something about your product. So try not to waste it! Make sure that you are relevant, interesting and prepared.

Be relevant

Remember: the purpose of your presentation is to show that your product meets the *specific need of the buyer*. You must, therefore, concentrate only on those parts of your product that meet this need.

Thus, if your product has additional benefits, or can do other things which are not strictly relevant to the buyer's need, ignore them. Wasting time describing irrelevant benefits can cost you dear. Only when you have completed your presentation and matched what your product can do with the buyer's needs, can you then begin to think of mentioning these additional features.

Be interesting

As explained in Chapter 4, you must always make an effort to interest your listener. So, for example, when you present your product, choose situations which are interesting and understandable to your listener. Paint a verbal picture for him. Let him actually 'see' the product in action, as it were. If nothing else, you will at least have his attention.

To put it another way: try to avoid droning on about the incredible features of your product and the benefits your listener will reap by buying it. He will only switch off if you do. So go one step further: bring your product to life and make it sound interesting.

Be prepared

Selling is a competitive business. If you want to succeed in it, then you too must be ready to compete.

Among other things, this means that you should be nothing less than word-perfect in your presentation of your product. You should know all your facts, you should be able to express the benefits of those facts and you should have the answers to most of the objections which your listener is likely to raise.

To be specific, when you pick up the phone to speak to your buyer, you must be prepared to answer just about anything the buyer might throw at you. For example, all your important information (your product data, your arguments and your answers to difficult questions) should be written down in note form and laid out in front of you.

Unfortunately, as you will quickly discover when you start selling, having the relevant information in front of you is one thing, being able to refer to it instantly is another.

Suppose, for example, you prepare an answer to a difficult question in advance. The following day a buyer asks you that precise question. As you hear it coming, you glance down at your notes to find the reply. What do you see? A mass of jottings, comments and scribbled information, but no sign of your precious and carefully prepared riposte. The buyer has now finished asking the question and is expecting an answer. Oh dear! Of course, you do your best but your listener is not impressed and bang goes your sale.

The moral of this tale is simple. If, as is usually the case, you need to rely on notes when selling, make sure that they are accessible immediately and digestible at a glance.

The 'box' method

This is a simple way of making your notes more available when you are deep in conversation. It is especially useful for sales beginners.

Basically, it involves *dividing up* your most important notes into bite-sized pieces and putting them into individual *boxes*. These boxes should be drawn out on a sheet of paper in front of you, for easy recognition and reference. In addition, no box should contain more than one basic 'point', 'idea' or 'answer'. This way you can not only see, at a glance, what the box is about but you can also instantly absorb its message even when you are talking. The only exception to this last rule is where you have a chunk of data that relates only to one point (for example, statistics that show the reliability of your product, or statistics which show how cost-effective your product is, and so on). Here, the data may all go into one box.

Examples of boxes you could prepare are as follows:

1. Key product benefit no 1
2. Key fact no 1 (to back up benefit no 1)
3. Key product benefit no 2
4. Key fact no 2
5. Key product benefit no 3
6. Key benefit fact no 3
7. Key product benefit no 4
8. Key fact no 4
9. Data chunk A (a chunk of data to give extra support to the above benefits)
10. Data chunk B (data about product reliability)
11. Key customers (names of those who already buy from you; these should be listed according to type/size of business)
12. Key potential customers (names of those who are almost certain to buy from you shortly)
13. Key advantage over competitor no 1
14. Key advantage over competitor no 2
15. Key advantage over competitor no 3
16 Data chunk C (data about your competitors)
17. Key answer to standard objection A (plus supporting fact)
18. Key answer to standard objection B (plus supporting fact)
19. Key answer to standard objection C (plus supporting fact)
20. Data chunk D (data concerning your company)
21. Key 'hold on tight' questions (× 2) (see p 65)
22. Key 'if-questions' (× 2) (see p 81)
23. Key probing questions (× 2) (see p 92)
24. Key closing questions (× 2) (see Chapter 9)

Obviously, this list can be expanded or adapted to fit your particular sales needs.

Ideally, your boxes should all be drawn out on a large single sheet of paper and arranged *in order of use* for optimum visual effect. For example, all your benefit boxes should be arranged in sequence with their respective fact boxes alongside.

One final point: do not be put off by the work involved in designing all these boxes. You will find these a great help when you are under pressure in the heat of the moment.

What you must do

● Now that the buyer has told you his need, you must proceed to satisfy it. You must explain how your product can do the job that needs to be done or can solve the problem that needs to be solved.

● As you will see from the examples below, exactly how you go about it will depend upon the product you are selling and the story behind it. It will also, to a great extent depend on the reaction of your listener. He may, for example, insist that you focus on certain issues, or he may try to disrupt your flow (and thus impose himself) by asking awkward or pedantic questions. Either way, you may find yourself having to alter your intended presentation and improvise as you go along.

Ideally, however, your presentation should go something like this:

● A brief explanation of the background of your product and/or your company.

● A brief but interesting explanation of how your product meets the buyer's need. This must stress benefits rather than facts.

● A brief explanation of how cost-effective your product is, when compared either with rival products or with what it can do for the buyer. Where necessary, use an 'interesting' statistic: one that 'means' something to the listener.

Note that when objections are raised during your presentation, try to postpone answering them until the right moment. Tell your buyer that you will deal with them 'in a moment'! This is usually not too difficult to do, as we shall see in the examples below.

I must emphasize, though, that the best way of avoiding objections is to make sure that you present your product in an interesting and relevant fashion.

Example No 1 (continued from p 79)

Salesperson: OK. Well let me deal with the service side of things first. To begin with, because we're larger and probably deal with a lot more customers than your local supplier, we've got the resources to make it easy for you to deal with us. For example, you don't have to ring us, we ring you. In fact, we'll arrange to ring you once a week – or more often if you prefer that – at whatever time suits you. As well as that, the person who rings you will know exactly what they are talking about. So if you're worried about product compatibility, for instance, they'll tell you what's compatible and what isn't. If you've heard about a new product, for example, the chances are first, that they'll know about it, and second, that we'll be getting it in stock. What I'm really saying is that we want to make life as easy for you as we can.

Buyer: But what about when you run out of stock?

Salesperson: I'll come to that in just a moment. OK, we ring you once a week to take your order. It'll then be packed the same day and delivered by special courier 48 hours later. Now, if by chance you forget to put something urgent on your order, or you suddenly find you're going to run out of something, don't worry. You can always get through to us. We've got over 30 telephone lines, and we have an emergency overnight courier service to make sure that anything you order (up to 4 pm) will be delivered to you before lunchtime the following day. So basically, whatever your particular need is, we can fix it. Now you asked about out of stock problems?

Buyer: That's right. How often do you run out of stock?

Salesperson: You mean how often are we out of stocks of things like computer paper, typing paper, envelopes, typewriter ribbons, pens, that sort of thing? The things you need all the time?

Buyer: Yes.

Salesperson: Never.

Buyer: I don't believe it.

Salesperson: Well, check what we say in the brochure. You see all the items I mentioned are down in our catalogue as Grade A items. And all Grade A items are *always* in stock. That's

	why so many companies use us. And there's no magic to it, we just carry huge stocks of all the most common items. That's why we never run out.
Buyer:	What about less common items?
Salesperson:	Less common items are what we call Grade B stuff. They include things like specialized rubber stamps, certain types of expandable files, electronic adding machines, and so on. Now, even as far as this stuff is concerned, we're rarely, if ever, out of stock. And even if we are, we guarantee to be in stock within three days, so in practice it's not a problem. I mean, to give you a concrete example, yesterday we sent out over 85 orders with about 1,000 items in them; and out of all of that, only one item was marked out of stock and that was one of our 'top of the range' adding machines. Now that's not bad, is it?
Buyer:	No, not bad.
Salesperson:	Right, so the service *works*. It's reliable, it's easy and it doesn't break down because of out-of-stock problems. You won't, for example, find that we have to order items for you, to be delivered as and when we get round to it and you won't have any more worries about not being able to send out invoices because your printer's run out of paper. Now I call that a first-class service. How about you?
Buyer:	It's not bad. What about the money side of things?
Salesperson:	That's the second bit of good news. Because we buy in such large quantities, we get very good prices, which in turn, we pass onto you. For instance, what do you normally pay for an 'X' typewriter ribbon, just taking it as an example? I'd say probably about £4, excluding VAT?
Buyer:	About that.
Salesperson:	Well, for the 'X' ribbon, we charge £3.75, excluding VAT, but we also stock the 'Y' ribbon – which is every bit as good as the 'X', in practice – and that only costs £3.45. These are only examples. I could quote you dozens of others and every one of them would be a step lower than the prices you're paying at the moment. I mean, I'll be frank with you: it would be worth your while switching to us for the better service *alone*, never mind the lower

Buyer:

Salesperson:

prices. But when you can also save a fair amount of money on top of that, well, really, you'd be daft not to give us a try, wouldn't you?

Buyer:
It's worth thinking about anyway.

Salesperson:
OK. Well, before we go any further, can you think of anything I haven't covered? Is there anything else about the service which you want to know, which I haven't mentioned?

Buyer:
What about credit terms? I assume you give 30 days' credit as usual?

Salesperson:
Yes, that's all standard.

Buyer:
In that case, I think you've covered just about everything.

Note how you choose to start with a very practical and uncontroversial benefit. There is little here for the buyer to argue with and so you can be sure of a peaceful start.

Actually, your beginning is even more subtle than it first appears. Explaining how 'user-friendly' you are immediately defuses the standard criticism of larger companies – that their size prevents them from offering friendly, personal service. This criticism is bound to be in the back of the buyer's mind since the supplier he currently deals with is smaller, but probably very friendly. You have, therefore, done well to get your 'reassurance' in first.

Also, by focusing on your customer service, you succeed in flushing our another concern of your listener – how often are you out of stock? Getting this concern out into the open is doubly useful because, not only does it tend to show that the buyer is probably a little dissatisfied with the stock situation of his current supplier, but it also enables you to use the expressed concerned as a way of introducing your strongest benefit: the real reliability of your service. Overall, a good start.

Note also how you bring your story to life, in your first two 'speeches', by painting verbal pictures of typical phone call situations and typical business concerns. Even your emergency courier service is mentioned more to show how your company can handle an everyday office difficulty (running out of an important piece of stationery) rather than because you think the buyer will actually need the service in question. Incidentally, this is a good example of an exception to the normal rule of relevancy.

Note how you handle the out-of-stock question. You don't answer it outright; instead, you respond with a question of your own which enables you to qualify the original question before giving a definite reply – a good example of answering a question with a question.

Note also how once again you explain your stock situation in a relevant and imaginative way. You keep everything on a very practical level and continue to use simple, down-to-earth examples. Note also the language you use. For example, important Grade A stationery is referred to as 'items', whereas less important Grade B stationery is referred to as 'stuff'. In addition, by quoting only complicated or fairly irrelevant items – such as electronic adding machines and specialized rubber stamps – as examples of Grade B stuff, you further downgrade and marginalize their importance.

Note how you never mention facts or benefits on their own. One always leads to the other. For example, a fact (or facts) always leads to a benefit, or else a benefit is immediately supported by one or more facts or examples (such as 'We're larger ... we've got the resources (facts) to make it easy for you to deal with us' (benefit).

A small point: note the way you refer to your brochure. You never draw too much attention to it, in case the buyer postpones further discussion until he had read it. Nevertheless, you still refer to it occasionally to support the points you make.

Note the careful use of questions throughout your presentation to probe for listener reaction: (for example, 'Now that's not bad, is it?', 'I call that a first-class service. How about you?', 'What do you normally pay for ... ?', 'You'd be daft not to give us a try, wouldn't you?') You should always take care to check what your listener is thinking as you go. Do not simply talk *at* him.

Example No 2 (continued from p 81)

Salesperson: Well, just let me briefly explain the gist of our service – it'll only take a moment – and then you tell me what you think. Fair enough?

Buyer: Fair enough, but keep it brief. I haven't got all day.

Salesperson: OK. Very simply, what we do is to help hotels increase their profits by helping them to give their customers a better service. You see, five years ago we commissioned two national surveys. The first was a survey of 1000 hotels across the country, and the second was a survey of approximately 2000 hotel guests. These surveys showed two things: first, that most hotels ran their tea and coffee services at a loss – in other words, the returns hardly justified the cost of staff and so on – and second, that most hotel guests hated the normal sort of hotel coffee and were quite prepared to pay more, for more quality and more variety. And that's why Café Deluxe was set up: to help hotels give their customers a better service, which in turn the hotels could charge more for.

Buyer:	It all sounds good in theory, but has it worked in practice?
Salesperson:	Definitely. As it says in our brochure, we're now the market leader for the sorts of coffee we offer, we supply several of the larger- and medium-sized hotel chains plus we supply at least 250 of the independents. So it must be working fairly well. However, we also do another interesting thing – and this is also explained in the brochure. After three months, we ask every single one of our new customers to estimate the increase in profits they generate from selling our coffees. They are each asked to mark off a number on a scale of one to ten, (ten being the highest), and the average to date is seven. So there you are, the facts speak for themselves: when hotels start buying our coffee, their profits go up. Now isn't that the sort of thing you want, Mr Smith?
Buyer:	But how do I know it will work for me?
Salesperson:	Well, if you bear with me for a moment, I'll tell you.
	The first and most important thing we do for anyone who stocks our range of luxury coffees is to help them tell their customers about it. The coffees may be very high quality and may have won all sorts of awards, but none of this is important unless the people who come into your hotel know about it. They have to be tempted to buy them, after all.
	So we supply you with a complete set of upright table menus giving details of each individual coffee in the range. They explain things like where the coffees come from, how they are made, what they taste like, what awards they've won and so on. You can put these menus on all the tables in your Lounge, or in Reception – you can even put one in all your bedrooms; it's up to you. In addition, we also give you a full collection of small eye-catching signs to hang from the ceiling or on the walls. So, no matter where people sit, they'll notice the fact that your hotel serves a range of luxury coffees and they're bound to be tempted. That's when you start making money.
Buyer:	But what if they're not coffee drinkers?
Salesperson:	In general, that's not something you have to worry about. According to the latest consumer figures – which we quote in detail in our brochure – almost 95 per cent of

all adults over 21 drink coffee. In addition, 75 per cent of all men prefer drinking coffee to tea. Now, since I imagine that most of the commercial travellers staying with you are men, you can see that we're talking about a product which *already* appeals to the vast majority of your customers. By *improving* that product – by offering a luxury, fresh-tasting coffee instead of the usual 'instant' stuff, and by offering 20 completely different varieties instead of just one –I don't think you'll have any problems tempting your particular customers to taste it. Do you see what I mean?

Buyer: Yes, I follow.

Salesperson: Now, one more thing: because all the coffee is specially produced in sealed coffee bags, you can serve all your customers quickly without any of the usual mess and wastage you get from the old-fashioned filter coffees. So your guests get all the flavour and aroma of fresh coffee and all you have to do is boil a kettle. Now what could be simpler than that?

Buyer: OK, what's the cost?

Salesperson: Well, this is the interesting bit. As you know, serving someone coffee costs next to nothing in terms of what actually goes in the cup –the coffee, milk and sugar and so on. What costs the money is the time taken to make it, serve it, clear it away and wash it up. So, since your costs are always going to remain relatively low, the only way to increase your profits is to serve something which has a higher perceived value and which you can, therefore, charge more for. Now you said you normally charge between 70p and £1 for a cup of coffee, is that right?'

Buyer: Yes, that's right.

Salesperson: Well, the recommended selling price of our coffee varies from £1.50 to £1.85 depending on which coffee the customer selects, so you're almost doubling your takings straight away.

Buyer: [interrupting] But what does it cost *me*? The coffee, I mean.

Salesperson: Literally, a few extra pennies, that's all. Instead of paying about 2p a cup, which I imagine you probably do at the moment, you'll pay about 8p. That's an extra 6p on your costs in return for an extra 80p to £1 on your sales. And that includes all the menus, the signs and so on. Now that's not a bad deal, is it?

Buyer: No, it doesn't sound too bad.

In this example, because you are selling a relatively new type of product/ service, or at least one that is new to the buyer himself, you must try to explain some of the background involved.

If you simply charge in by explaining the details of the service, your listener is almost certain to question the idea behind it. He will probably reject the whole idea that customers want – and are prepared to pay extra for – a type of fancy coffee. You, therefore, begin your presentation by hurrying to reassure them on both counts.

Note how, as in the first example, you provoke an objection – 'Has it worked in practice?' – for which you are well prepared. Note the careful use of facts to support your benefit that your coffee boosts profits. You avoid submerging your listener in a sea of statistics and instead give him just the right amount to think about: your company is the market leader; a good number of hotels are paying to receive your service; and your customers themselves say that their profits have increased.

Look carefully at the buyer's next question, 'But how do I know it'll work for me?' It is typically awkward. On the face of it, he is asking for the impossible. After all, no salesperson can guarantee that his product will definitely work for a particular customer. The simple answer therefore is, 'You don't'. However, what the buyer really means is, 'How do I know it'll *probably* work for me?', or, 'Tell me something that will make be feel *confident* that the product will work for me,' This of course is very different, and it allows you to offer a standard part of your presentation in reply. You go straight into a practical, down-to-earth description of how you catch customers' attention. Once again, by anticipating the general type of question asked you are able to offer a fluent reply.

The same goes for the buyer's next objection, 'What if they're not coffee drinkers?' By preparing your reply, you can, once again, exploit the objection to further your case. Incidentally, if the buyer himself had not raised it, you would probably have raised it yourself anyway and then gone on to answer it in the same way.

Note how, as in the first example, you avoid mentioning price. This provokes the buyer into raising it himself and so you give a brief, simple explanation of how cost-effective your product is and how it boosts profits. Like the previous objections, if the buyer himself had not brought up the issue of price, then you would have, albeit possibly at a later stage.

Note finally, again as in the first example, both the way you refer to your sales brochure for confirmation and also the way you use questions for listener reaction. For example, 'Let me just briefly explain the gist of our service ... and then you tell me what you think. Fair enough?', 'Now isn't that the sort of thing you want, Mr Smith?', 'Do you see what I mean?', 'Now what could be simpler than that?', and, 'Now that's not a bad deal, is it?' Notice how each question is carefully phrased so that the only response is 'Yes'.

The 'suggestion' section

What you must do

- Having explained your product to your buyer and answered his immediate objections, you should now suggest that he *buys*. This suggestion is usually put in the form of a question.
- In the majority of cases, this suggestion to buy will trigger the standard reply, 'I'll have to think about it.'
- This can mean just about anything. It can be a 'Yes', a 'Maybe', a 'No' or even a 'Don't know'.
- In practice, the only thing you can do is to probe politely in order to find out which of these possibilities is nearest to the truth. Unless you are very confident of your ability, do not press the buyer *at this stage*. You have little to gain and much to lose.
- Ideally, you should probe for the truth by asking one or two fairly gentle questions, such as:

  'Is there anything you're not satisfied with?'
  'What's your reaction to what I've told you?'
  'Does everything sound all right, or are there one or two things you're not quite sure about?'
  'Look, people are always worried about something when it comes to spending money. What concerns you most about dealing with us/about what I've told you?'
  'How do you feel about what I've told you? Are you satisfied with everything, or is there something you're not quite sure about?'

  As you can see, they are all variations of the same theme: what does the buyer himself think about what you have said? Try thinking up your own questions and say them out loud to see how they sound.

How to speak
The emphasis is the same throughout the presentation call. Try to sound as positive and as assured as possible. Remember: you are asking your listener to spend money with you, so you must sound reliable.

One final point to bear in mind: when selling over the telephone, how you sound counts for almost as much as what you say. That is why it is always so important to prepare yourself for certain calls, because if you come across as hesitant or aggressive, you will quickly forfeit the trust of your listener and, with it, your chances of a sale.

Example No 1 (continued from p 87)

Salesperson: OK, so how about putting together a first order for us? That way we can actually show you how good we are. Can you get one prepared by Monday, for example:

Buyer: Hmmm. I'm not sure. I'll have to think about it first.

Salesperson: Sure, have a think about it. While I'm on the phone, though, can I ask you how you feel about what I've told you? Are you satisfied with everything or is there something you're not quite sure about?

Buyer: No, it all sounds pretty reasonable. I just need the weekend to think about it, that's all.

Salesperson: No problem. How about if I call you, say, first thing on Tuesday? We can go over anything I haven't mentioned then.

Buyer: Yes, that's fine.

Salesperson: OK, now finally, before I go, what about the big match on Saturday, the rugby international? Who do you fancy, England or Wales?

Buyer: Actually I can't stand rugby. Football is more my game.

Salesperson: Oh, which team do you follow?

Buyer: York City.

Salesperson: York City? Who are they? Are they some sort of amateur team?

Buyer: Cheeky beggar. They're top of the Fourth Division at the moment.

You should now bring the conversation to a close by reminding the buyer to expect a call from you first thing on Tuesday.

Note the carefully phrased suggestion-question. As you can see, it actually comprises two different questions with an assertion of reliability in between. The introduction of this assertion allows you to phrase your second question in a more direct manner – a useful technique.

Note your response to the reply, 'I'll have to think about it first'. You immediately probe for what lies behind this reply. Fortunately, because the buyer sounds fairly positive, you decide not to push too much.

Generally speaking, how you respond to the standard reply will depend upon your overall powers of persuasion. If you feel you can push the buyer for a decision and still extricate yourself if he bites back, all well and good. If you are not sure, keep your distance and just probe gently.

Note also how you end the conversation on a clever personal note. This not only extends your telephone rapport with your listener, it also gives you a useful future point of conversation: he hates rugby and supports York City Football Club. Incidentally, in case you are sceptical about the value of asking personal questions, let me tell you the following story.

Years ago, a young salesperson telephoned the person who was responsible for buying all the advertising for a major brand of cigars. This salesperson duly presented his product but to no avail; the buyer did not seem in the least bit interested. However, before ringing off, the salesperson happened to ask the buyer for his opinion about a forthcoming sporting event, only to discover that he was a passionate supporter of York City Football Club. Ten minutes of football talk later, the salesperson returned to the subject of advertising and was told to ring back the following day, on the off-chance that the buyer might be able to do business with him, after all. The salesperson duly rang back and the buyer bought £500-worth of advertising space. Indeed, this buyer continued to buy advertising space from the salesperson for the next nine months: a total of approximately £5000-worth. This incident happened to me early in my career. I have never forgotten the lesson it contained and I have applied it to great effect, ever since.

Example No 2 (continued from p 91)

Salesperson:	OK, let me tell you how we arrange things. It's all very easy. We do three different starter packs. They contain everything a hotel needs to start offering our luxury coffee service. They include a complete set of the 20 individual coffees, plus a complete package of table menus, signs and so on. They only vary in the amount of coffee they contain, that's all.
Buyer:	And how much are they?
Salesperson:	The de luxe starter pack is £500, the middle of the range pack is £250 and our standard pack is £150. And in each case, as I said, it works out at about 8p a cup. So, for example, assuming you only sell 40 cups a day, which would obviously be quite low, the cheapest pack will give you about six weeks' supply. In practice, though, you will be back to me well before then. I mean, usually, as soon as a hotel starts offering this sort of coffee service to its customers, they go mad. The customers, I mean. They all start ordering coffee and the hotel manager usually comes back to me, within a

	fortnight at the latest, to reorder stocks. It's good business, believe me.
Buyer:	Hmmm.
Salesperson:	So how do you want to start? Which starter pack do you want?
Buyer:	I'm not really sure. Let me have a chat with the wife and give me a ring on Monday.
Salesperson:	She isn't a fanatical tea drinker is she, by any chance?
Buyer:	Oh no, nothing like that. If anything, she is the coffee drinker in the family.
Salesperson:	Good, I'm glad to hear it. OK, before I go, is there anything you're not satisfied with? Anything that doesn't sound quite right?
Buyer:	No. I think most of what you've said sounds reasonable. I just want some time to go over a few things, that's all.
Salesperson:	Well, have a look at our brochure over the weekend; it explains everything very thoroughly and it should answer any questions you might have, which I haven't dealt with. And I'll ring you about 3.00 on Monday. How's that?
Buyer:	That's fine.

You now bring the conversation to a close.

Note that, unlike the first example, you still have some work to do before asking your customer to buy. This is not unusual when it comes to selling someone a product which he does not currently stock.

The particular approach used here is the 'starter-pack routine'. Very often, if a customer does not stock a particular product range, he will be offered a starter pack of the product containing a few of all the items in the range. This enables him to start selling the whole range immediately. Then, once the items start to sell, he can come back and reorder them individually or in smaller quantities, according to what sells best. These starter packs usually come in three or more basic sizes: large, medium and small.

The 'starter-pack routine' (or 'close') requires you to explain first what starter packs the customer *can* buy and then to ask which one he *will* buy. Alas, in this example, the buyer manages to escape by asking for time to think about it.

Incidentally, note how the three differently priced starter packs are introduced to the listener. It is a good example of how to introduce the customer to products of different value. You *always* start with your most expensive product, followed by the less expensive ones in sequence. This means that, by the time you get to your cheapest product, it really does seem like a bargain. Even where you *know* that your customer cannot possibly afford your top price products, you must still observe this rule. The more outrageous and expensive your top product sounds, the more of a bargain your lowest one will sound by comparison.

Note, finally, your response to the buyer's request for more time: you probe for what might lie behind it. The buyer seems to be fairly positive, so you avoid pressing too much.

9. How to Close

So far, we have dealt with the first four problems that must be overcome if you wish to sell something to a company over the phone.

You have learned, for example:

- How to find out the name of the buyer.
- How to get through to him.
- How to introduce yourself and canvass him.
- How to present your product to him and deal with his immediate objections.

We now come to the fifth and final problem – getting the buyer to actually buy the product – something which is known universally throughout the sales world as 'closing'.

Closing is the process of final persuasion, the process of overcoming all the buyer's final objections and getting him to take a decision to buy your product. It may take one telephone call, it may take two or even three different calls, spread out over a week or ten days or even longer, but the emphasis is always the same. *It is time for the buyer to take a decision.*

How closing fits into the overall sales process

Before we deal with the mechanics of how to close a sale, we must first understand how it fits into the overall sales process.

Closing is the climax of the whole sales process

Ultimately, the whole point of telephoning a buyer is to get him to buy your product.

This is not to say that all your other work is unimportant. Far from it. Unless you successfully canvass your buyer and then present your product to him in a relevant and interesting way, you will never even get a chance to close the sale. What it does mean, though, is that, by themselves, these other things are not enough; you have to go on to clinch the sale.

To put it another way, you must maintain the right attitude. You must never forget that all your efforts must constantly be directed towards getting your buyer to agree to spend money on your product. Whatever else he does is irrelevant. In short, you must always remember that you are paid to get him to buy.

In this connection, please note the following:

Be the buyer's business partner not his friend
As explained in Chapter 5, you should always try to establish a rapport with the 'human being' at the end of the phone, rather than just the 'voice', and, indeed, this is very important for all sorts of reasons. However, this personal approach should never blind you to the fact that the only reason you speak to a buyer is to do business with him.

In other words, friendship with a buyer always flows from the business you do with him, not the other way around. Never make the mistake of thinking that a buyer will start buying from you because he likes you.

'Sales talk, excuses walk'
This is one of the oldest sayings in the world of sales. It means that, as a salesperson, you are only ever judged or assessed on the number of actual sales you make.

'Very-nearly sales', or 'almost-but-not-quite-sales', or even 'he-would-have-bought-but-for-the-money sales' are utterly irrelevant. What counts are real-life, actual sales, the sort your company can charge money for.

Who is the best salesperson?
The best salesperson is not the person with the greatest capacity for hard work, nor is he the one with the most important customers. Nor is he the person with the most persistence, the funniest jokes, the most confidence, the most energy or the most charisma. He is not even the person with the best telephone manner.

The best salesperson is the person with the most *sales*.

The more customers you talk to the more you will close
You will never close all your sales. In fact, the chances are that you will never close more than a small proportion of the buyers to whom you speak. There is just too much competition, too many buyers with fixed ideas and too many invisible obstacles lurking in the background, to allow you to do much more.

You an conduct a series of exemplary sales calls only to find that you are turned down at the last moment for any one of a number of reasons.

For example, a competitor may nip in ahead of you and massively undercut your price; or your buyer may suddenly be told to stop spending money by his senior management. You may even discover, at the end of the day, that your friendly, trustworthy buyer never really intended to buy from you at all; either, unknown to you, he retains some sort of prejudice against your product or your company, or he was just putting out feelers to see what he could get for his money.

In short, you are involved in a constant battle against the odds and against all sorts of obstacles, both visible and invisible.

So learn how to improve the odds
I mention all these pitfalls and obstacles not to depress you, but to show you that, when it comes to persuading people to part with their money, life can be painful and unpredictable.

To give you another more specific example: you can easily set up closing calls to four different customers, who have each promised to buy, say, £500-worth of your product, only to find when you call them back that one is away, another has forgotten to clear it with his managing director, another has changed his mind ('very sorry and all that') while one has decided to start with a more modest order worth £50. As you can imagine, this sort of disaster does nothing either for your self-esteem or for your reputation within your company, 'Sales talk, excuses walk', remember?

So what is the answer? How can you minimize the chances of this happening to you? Well, it really all comes down to numbers and it involves the whole sales process – canvassing calls, presentation calls, closing calls, the lot.

The numbers game
The more customers you canvass, the more customers you can get to listen to your presentation. And the more customers you can get to listen to your presentation, the more you can convince to spend money with you.

So, for example, if you canvass 100 customers, you may find that 60 are receptive and worth pursuing. When you then present your product to this group of 60, you may find that five change their mind and do not wish to listen to you, five you can never get through to, 20 turn you down flat once they hear the details of your product, and 30 all say, 'I'll have to think about it.' You duly ring back these 30 remaining customers in order to deal with their final objections and close the sale and perhaps ten turn you down flat, 15 want more time to think about it and five actually buy. Finally, out of the 15 who wanted more time, nine cannot or will not come to a decision while six buy.

Result
Out of 100 customers canvassed, only 11 finally buy. Furthermore, it is difficult to predict in advance which of these original 100 will make up the final 11. They may conceivably be the first 11 customers whom you canvassed, they may even be the last 11 you canvassed, or they may come from somewhere in between.

Assuming the same rate of success (11 per cent), it is clear that if you wish to sell to 55 customers, you have to canvass 500 customers first.

You can see that the more customers you contact, the more you are likely to be able to close and the more actual sales you will make. In addition, by increasing the quantity of customers whom you contact, you are, in effect, insuring yourself against the unforeseen problems and obstacles which can crop up at the last moment and ruin your chances.

How to close a sale

The problem
In simple terms, the main problem about closing a sale is that while you want the buyer to take a decision to buy your product – and to take that decision now – he may have other ideas.

For example, not only is he likely to have several last minute doubts and objections about going ahead with the deal, he is also likely to resist having to take a decision on the spot.

Your task is, therefore, twofold: first, to convince the buyer that he needs your product by answering any objections he has to buying it; and secondly, to politely but firmly get him to come to a decision and commit himself.

The solution
So how do you overcome a buyer's objections and convince him to buy?

This is the most difficult question in the whole book. Unfortunately, there is no guaranteed method of persuading anyone to buy your product, far less a method of getting them to say 'Yes' there and then.

Nevertheless, one has to start somewhere. I, therefore, suggest that you adopt the following method as a basic guide to the problem.

It is called the '*sandwich*' method of closing.

The 'sandwich' method of closing

Closing is all about getting a purchase order from your buyer. When you ring him, therefore, in order to close the deal, you must focus on this issue of the order and handle things in the following sequence:

First, after introducing yourself in the normal way, you must explain to him that you are ringing to take his order. You must politely *push* for a positive decision. Above all, you must not sound as though you have an open mind on the subject. Instead, sound as though you assume he is going to buy – the only question being how much.

Second, when the buyer says (as he usually does) that he has doubts about going ahead, you must find out what these doubts are and answer them. In other words, you must overcome his objections.

Third, once you have resolved these objections, you must again *push* for a commitment to buy. Never expect the buyer to buy simply because his doubts have disappeared.

In simple terms, therefore, the sandwich method of closing involves:

1. Pushing for the order (at the start)
2. Overcoming any objections to the order
3. Pushing for the order (at the end).

Pushing for the order (at the start)
The most important thing here is to sound positive from the word go. Remember: you are ringing to close the sale and to get the buyer to spend money with you. You must, therefore, sound confident about your product and confident that the buyer has decided to buy it. Sound as though you assume that he is going to go ahead with the deal – once any remaining technical details have been sorted out – and that the only real question is how much he is going to spend.

Do not ask things like:

'Have you come to a decision yet, Mr Smith?'
'Do you want to go ahead with the purchase?'
'Have you had a chance to go through everything yet?'

All these questions hand the initiative to your listener and invite the answer 'No'.

Instead, say things like:

'I'm ringing to sort out which one you want.'
'I'm really calling to sort out your order for us, so I can get it off to you before the weekend.'
'I'm really calling to sort out any last minute details and to help you put together a first order for us.'
'I'm calling to go over any final points and arrange an order with you.'
'I'm calling to finalize what we discussed last week, so that we can sort out an order.'
'Is there anything you want to go over, before giving me the order?'

These positive statements create the sort of positive tone which buyers sometimes find hard to resist. Even if (as is more usual) a buyer does decline to go ahead, you may then confidently tackle his objections without losing the initiative.

Overcoming any objections to the order
This is the difficult bit. Buyers are not always renowned for their open-mindedness, especially if they have been in the job a number of years. Even after politely listening to your presentation and accepting that they could do with your product, a number of them still end up rejecting it because of prejudice or because they think they know better.

Fortunately, however, many buyers are fairly straightforward. They worry about perfectly understandable things like whether your product is too expensive for what it does, whether it really will do what you say it will, whether it is reliable; or how they are going to squeeze yet more money out of their already depleted budgets to pay for it and so on.

Whatever their objection, it is your job to overcome it as best you can and convince them to give you an order.

To do this, I recommend that you adopt the following easy-to-remember method.

The 'West Point Training Academy' method
This has nothing to do with the United States Military College of the same name. It is simply a phrase to help you remember how to handle objections.

'West' stands for 'Welcome'
'Point' stands for 'Probe'
'Training' stands for 'Test'
'Academy' stands for 'Answer'

Welcome
When a buyer tells you, for example, that your product is not reliable enough, do *not* rush in and try to answer the point immediately. You will only get his back up and lose the sale. Instead, *welcome* the objection. Say something like, 'I'm glad you've mentioned that', or, 'Yes, I agree that's a very important issue.'

By welcoming his objection, you are relaxing him, you are making him feel good and – most importantly – you are not letting him steal the initiative.

Probe
Having welcomed the buyer's objection, you quickly ask one or two questions in order to probe for the extent of the objection. In other words, you must get him to explain and clarify exactly what he means by it. Depending on the issue raised, ask him something like:

'Can you be a little more precise?'

'When you say the product is too expensive, what exactly do you mean?'
'What level of reliability are you looking for?'
'What sort of performance do you expect?'
'What are your minimum requirements here?'
'What exactly do you mean when you say it's not really what you're looking for?'

The point to remember is that you must not jump in and start answering the buyer's objection until you have found out exactly what he is objecting to and what he expects from you.

Example
Imagine you are selling advertising space in a local newspaper to the owner of a firm of estate agents. You call to close the deal only to find that your buyer has decided not to go through with it. He says, 'It's too expensive.' After welcoming this objection you should probe as follows:

Salesperson: When you say it's too expensive, Mr Smith, what exactly do you mean?

Buyer: Just that, it's too expensive.

Salesperson: Do you mean that you are worried in case not enough people see your advertisement?

Buyer: Partly.

Salesperson: Are you worried in case not enough people reply or respond to the advertisement?

Buyer: Basically, yes.

Salesperson: So, in other words, you're worried that you won't get the results you're looking for?

Buyer: Yes.

Salesperson: Right, I understand. Now, I presume that anyone looking for a house can walk into your office and browse through the house details on display?

Buyer: That's right.

Salesperson: And If they find something of interest, they can ask for a copy of the details and take it away without having to explain who they are, or what they're looking for and so on. Is that right?'

Buyer: Yes.

Salesperson: So it's quite common for people to pass in and out of

> your offices without being quizzed in any way by your staff?'

Buyer:　　　Yes.

Result

You have clarified the buyer's objection. When he said that advertising with you was 'too expensive', he really meant that he was afraid the results would not justify the expense.

You have also discovered, however, that he has no standard procedure for finding out why many people use his estate agency when they are looking for houses.

In other words, it could be because they have seen his previous advertisements in the paper or because of the convenient location of his offices or for one of a number of different reasons.

Your probing has, therefore, clarified his complaint and has also generated a possible line of response as follows.

To begin with you should obviously quote certain official details about the number of people who buy your paper and respond to its advertisements. You should also remind the customer of the number of his competitors who advertise with you. After all, if overall business is down, it becomes even more important to fight for the business that remains.

You should then tell him that, in all probability, a significant amount of his current business is actually the result of his previous advertising with you. He is in no position to dispute this because he has no standard procedure for finding out why many of his customers use his agency. He seems to make no attempt to monitor the results of his advertising. Your probing has worked very well.

Test

Having welcomed the objection and having probed for clarification, you should still hold your fire until you have *tested* it. It may not be the buyer's real objection at all. It may be an excuse or a cover for what is really bothering him.

If you do go ahead and answer a fake objection, you will waste precious time and achieve nothing. So hold your fire and test the objection first. *The best way of doing this is to ask an 'if-question' along the following lines*:

> 'If I can show you that the product meets your standards of reliability, can I assume that you'll go ahead with the deal?
> 'If I can show you that the product is at least as cost-effective as the one you've been using up to now, will that satisfy you?'
> 'If I solve the delivery problem for you, can I take it that you'll buy?'
> 'If I can help you get around your budget problem, will you go ahead with the deal?'

Questions like these will normally provoke the buyer into showing his hand.

Either he will say 'Yes' to you, thus confirming the genuineness of his objection – in which case you can proceed immediately to the 'Answer' section below – or he will bluster for a moment or two and then tell you what his real worry is, in which case you can simply repeat the process.

Answer
Only after you have welcomed the objection, probed it for clarification and then tested it to find out if it is really genuine, should you try to answer it.

OK, so how do you go about answering?

Make sure that you are fully prepared
The vast majority of objections raised are neither new nor unexpected. Indeed, they are nearly always standard objections along the lines of *cost* ('Your product is too expensive for what it does'), or *performance* ('Your product will not do what I want it to do'), or *reliability* ('I don't trust your product to keep working', or, 'I don't trust your company to be able to provide the necessary after-sales service').

You should, therefore, be *well prepared* for such objections and you should have the answers ready – if not in your head then at least on the desk in front of you.

For example, if the objection concerns cost, you should be able to marshal your facts and your evidence to show that your product is at least as cost-effective as any of its rivals. If you have to go into detail to do this, that is fine. Just remember to keep everything as clear as you can. Allow the facts to clarify your point not confuse it.

I have stressed throughout this book that preparation is vital. Now you can see why. If you are fully prepared to answer these sorts of standard objection, you will always close more sales than someone who has not bothered to make the effort.

Be ready to restate your main benefits and supporting facts
If and when a buyer remains unconvinced with your answer to his objection or hesitates about going ahead with the deal, you must step in and restate your main benefits and the facts that support them.

You must remind the buyer of the strength and suitability of your product and try to present all the relevant facts which show that your product can deliver most, if not all, of the benefits he is looking for.

Persevere
Never be afraid of repeating yourself or of going over the same arguments several times.

Be patient, persevere and never take 'No' for an answer, unless you feel you have something to gain by doing it. Keep calling back, if necessary. As long as you keep the deal alive, by refusing to take 'No' for an answer, you stand a chance of closing the sale.

Pushing for the order (at the end)

As soon as you feel that you have overcome your buyer's objections, you must once again push for a decision by suggesting that he buys.

Again, as we said at the beginning of the call, you must be positive in your approach. Simply asking your buyer if he wants to go ahead is not enough. You must steer him into accepting your proposition and giving you the order.

There are several ways of doing this and they are known in the sales world as 'closes': ways of closing a sale and getting the order.

Sometimes, you can get away with using just one type of close. More often than not, however, you use two or more, because the first one you try does not work on your particular buyer!

Study these closes carefully. Practise role-playing them. Try to understand them. They are all ways of reducing the buyer's ability to say 'No' while, simultaneously, increasing the likelihood of him saying 'Yes'.

The five closes

We will look at five of these closes as follows:

1. The assumptive close
2. The alternative close
3. The what-have-you-got-to-lose close
4. The incentive close
5. The what-on-earth close

The alternative close is illustrated fully in the examples at the end of this chapter, page 108.

The assumptive close

This works well when the product in question is clearly defined and where the buyer is hesitating about taking a final decision. It is best illustrated with an example. Suppose you are selling exhibition space at a forthcoming exhibition to a local company.

Buyer: It all sounds pretty reasonable ... but I'm not sure.

Salesperson: Well, time is pressing, Mr Smith, I think I'd better put you down for the space we've been talking about and get our stand-fitters to contact you next week; otherwise we run the risk of excluding your company altogether. Now who's going to be handling things at your end?

As you can see, no attempt is made to ask the buyer whether, in fact, he wants to go ahead: you simply *assume* he will. The only thing you ask is who your stand-fitters should contact.

This assumptive close can be watered down to suit more strong-minded customers, but its best effect is on the more uncertain type of person.

The alternative close

This is a very useful close for all types of situation and nearly all types of buyer.

The point of the close is that you do not ask the buyer, for example, whether he wants the blue product, but, instead, you ask him whether he wants the blue one or the red one. As you can see, whichever one he chooses, he ends up buying from you. This may sound a bit cheeky, but in fact it often has the effect of relaxing a buyer. He no longer has a massive decision to take, because you have taken it for him. All he has to do is to decide a relatively minor issue like, what size, what colour, or what extras he wants.

The what-have-you-got-to-lose close

This is another very useful close to have up your sleeve. It is certainly a good approach to fall back on when you meet a fairly intransigent buyer who keeps on saying 'No' for no good reason.

As the name suggests, your line of argument should run something like this:

The risks to him and his company, of going ahead with the purchase are minimal. Why, then, is he still refusing to buy when he has little or nothing to lose?

One of the nice things about this close is that you can make these points quite forcefully – usually without running the risk of offending your listener – and put quite a lot of pressure on your buyer, either to accept what you say and buy, or at least to explain what is bothering him. Of course, once you know what is bothering him, you then have a chance of resolving it and thus closing the sale.

The incentive close

As the name suggests, this is where you offer something extra to the buyer as an incentive to buy *now* rather than later.

In many cases, the skill here is to *appear* to give something away without actually doing so.

Where, however, you do give something away, you should try to take full advantage of it, either by using it to attract a brand-new customer or to get a regular customer to spend more money with you than usual. In other words, do not use your incentive as a substitute for selling.

The what-on-earth close
When you have tried everything you know to get the buyer to give you an order and still he refuses, try using the what-on-earth close.

The idea of it is to make a direct appeal to the buyer to explain why he is not buying.

It does not always work, by any means, but sometimes the message does get through and the buyer will tell you what he is really concerned about. Definitely worth a try if you meet a buyer who keeps saying 'No'.

Example

Salesperson:	OK. I've reassured you about our service, I've demonstrated how reliable we are and I've explained how we are less expensive than any of our competitors. And yet, you still insist that the product is not good enough for you. So tell me honestly, Mr Smith, what on earth do I have to do in order to get you to buy from us?

Conclusion
The real difficulty in practice about closing is knowing how hard to push your point of view.

For example, if you are not sufficiently robust in your explanation of why your buyer ought to buy, you are unlikely to convince him. On the other hand, if you are too robust or too dogmatic, you run the risk of irritating him and putting him off altogether.

Also, when should you push your point all the way and when should you cut your losses and arrange to call back another time?

These are difficult questions which only time and experience will help you to answer.

The alternative close

Example No 1 (continued from p 93)

Salesperson:	Hello, Mr Smith. I hope you had a good weekend. It's Sarah Brown here from Easiprint, the stationers. If you remember, we spoke at the end of last week.
Buyer:	Oh, yes.
Salesperson:	I said I'd call you this morning in order to go over anything I didn't mention last time and take your first order. How are things looking?
Buyer:	Actually I haven't really had a chance to decide what I'm going to do yet. Perhaps you could leave it with me until next week sometime.

Salesperson: I could do, but wouldn't the best thing be to actually show you our service *in practice?*[1]

Buyer: How do you mean?

Salesperson: Well, I think I told you all about our service last time. I explained how we guarantee always to be in stock of the items you need. I also went over our prices with you, which, from memory, were quite a bit lower than the ones you are paying at the moment. So you've *got* all the information: the only thing that remains now is for us to demonstrate our service in practice. So why not draw up a small order for us and put us to the test?[2] I mean, as they say, actions speak louder than words.

Buyer: I'm not sure.

Salesperson: Well, let's start with a couple of things you always need. Say, typewriter ribbons and computer paper. You said last time that you pay roughly £4 a ribbon. How much do you pay for your computer paper – about £3.50 a box?

Buyer: Er ... no. About £3.20.

Salesperson: And would I be right in assuming that you get through about ten ribbons and 50 boxes of paper a fortnight?

Buyer: About that.

Salesperson: Right, now I'm just doing some calculations at this end, because I want you to see the difference *in practice* between using us and using anyone else. If you buy ten 'X' ribbons – the sort you normally use – and 50 boxes of standard-width computer paper from your normal supplier, then, according to the figures you've given me, you pay £40 for your ribbons and £160 for your paper, which makes a total of £200. However, if you give me an order for exactly the same items, your company will only pay a total of £180 – that's a saving of 10 per cent or £20 on just one order. Enough to buy another seven boxes of computer paper.[3] Now surely, Mr Smith, when your company can save that much money on just one order, isn't it worth giving us a try?

---

[1] You have anticipated the buyer's reaction and you respond with this prepared answer.
[2] You continue to push.
[3] A good example of how to use facts to support your benefits.

At this point, the buyer will react in one of two ways. Either (1) he will begin to appreciate the logic of what you are saying and grudgingly recognize that his interests are best served by giving you a trial order, or (2) he will stand his ground and continue to hold out. These reactions are dealt with in sequence. In both cases the salesperson employs the 'alternative' method of closing the sale.

1. The buyer gives way

Buyer: I see what you mean.

Salesperson: Well, let me make a suggestion. Why don't we both put the whole thing to the test? Either let me put together an order for you – say just the ten ribbons and the 50 boxes of paper we talked about a moment ago – or, alternatively, you put one together yourself and I'll call back in half an hour to take the details. Tell me which option you prefer, and we can then get on with things and let our service speak for itself.[4]

Buyer: Hmmm. I think it's probably better if I do the order. There may be one or two other things we need.

Salesperson: Fine. How about if I call you in about half an hour?

Buyer: OK. I should have it ready for you by then.

You have closed the sale.

2. The buyer stand his ground and objects

Buyer: I'm still not sure. Price isn't everything.

Salesperson: I agree, price by itself may not be important at all.[5] In fact, in this case, I get the feeling that you're more concerned about the actual service we offer, rather than our prices. Am I right?[6]

Buyer: Yes.

Salesperson: Does this mean, though, that if I reassure you that our service can genuinely give you everything you could reasonably expect from a supplier, then you'll be happy to deal with us? That the service plus the low prices will put your mind at rest?[7]

---

[4] An example of how to 'create' an order for your buyer. You do not wait for him to suggest what to buy: you do it *for* him.

[5] You welcome the objection.

[6] You probe briefly for clarification.

[7] You test to see if the buyer's concern about reliability is genuine.

Buyer:	I suppose so, yes.
Salesperson:	OK, well let's focus for a moment on what can go wrong with the service and I'll see if I can reassure you about a few things.[8] Are you worried about us being out of stock, for example?
Buyer:	Yes, that is a worry.
Salesperson:	Well, you can now stop worrying. I don't know what your present supplier is like, but at Easiprint we just don't have that problem. As I explained last time, we operate a very strict system of stock control and we genuinely have huge stocks of all the basic stationery items. Now in practice, 90 per cent of all your orders will be for this sort of basic stationery – or what we call Grade A items – and we guarantee *never* to be out of stock of any of it. I mean, you can't ask more than that can you?
Buyer:	Not really, I suppose.
Salesperson:	As far as the less common items are concerned, as I've said, we hardly ever run out of stock of these either, and, if we do, we guarantee to have them back in stock within three working days. Now I assume that puts your mind at rest regarding stock problems?
Buyer:	Hmmm ... I think so.
Salesperson:	What about delivery, is that a worry too?
Buyer:	Well, since you're not local, yes it is.
Salesperson:	OK, once again you can relax because there is nothing to worry about. We use a first-class courier service and we guarantee delivery anywhere south of Birmingham within 48 hours. Plus, if it's urgent, we can deliver anything you order before 4 pm by lunchtime the following day.
Buyer:	And how much does this delivery cost?
Salesperson:	For all orders of £20 or more our standard delivery is completely free.
Buyer:	Hmmm.
Salesperson:	Now, tell me what else you're not absolutely sure about.

---

[8] Finally, you answer the objection. You do this by deliberately raising the issues involved and answering them one by one.

Buyer:	What about if something is damaged or faulty?
Salesperson:	No problem. Just send it back. You get a credit straight away.
Buyer:	[Says nothing.]
Salesperson:	Anything else?
Buyer:	Not that I can think of.
Salesperson:	Right. I've shown you how using us will save you money. I trust that now I have also put your mind at rest about our service and how it functions in practice. So I've done *my* bit. Now all *you* have to do is to give me a trial order and put us to the test. How about it?[9]
Buyer:	[pausing for a moment] Well, I suppose it all sounds reasonable.
Salesperson:	OK, well what's the best thing to do? Do you want *me* to put together an order for *you* – say the ten ribbons and the 50 boxes of computer paper we talked about earlier – or would you prefer to do one yourself and have me call back in half an hour to take the details?[10]
Buyer:	I suppose you might as well do the order. Make it for five ribbons, though, and 30 boxes of paper and we'll see about anything else afterwards.
Salesperson:	That's fine, Mr Smith. I'll do the order now myself and you'll have it on Thursday.

You have closed the sale.

Example No 2 (continued from p 95)

Salesperson:	Hello, Mr Jones, I hope you had a good weekend, it's Frank James here from Café Deluxe, the luxury coffee people. If you remember, we spoke at the end of last week.
Buyer:	Oh, yes.
Salesperson:	Now, I said I'd call you this afternoon in order to answer any final questions you may have about ordering our coffee. Is there anything you want to go over, anything

---

[9] Your suggestion, that the buyer should put you to the test, has been planned and thought out in advance.

[10] As in the previous example, you 'create' an order for your buyer. Even at this stage you avoid leaving it to the buyer to decide what he will buy.

you're not sure about, before we go ahead with the order?

Buyer: Yes, there is, actually. I've had a think about the whole thing and I'm really not sure that the idea will work for us here. I don't think it'll work in this hotel.

Salesperson: That's a perfectly understandable reaction, Mr Jones.[11] But tell me, what exactly do you mean when you say you don't think it'll work in your hotel? What basically concerns you?[12]

Buyer: I suppose I don't think that our customers are the sort to spend £1.80, or whatever, on a cup of coffee.

Salesperson: You don't think they've got the cash to spend, is that it?[12]

Buyer: No, they've got the money. It's just that I can't see them spending it on a cup of coffee.

Salesperson: You mean you think they'll quite happily spend £1.80 on a pint or a Bacardi and Coke but not on a coffee, is that it.[12]

Buyer: Exactly.

Salesperson: OK, well let me ask you this Mr Jones: if I can show you in fairly clear terms that your customers will buy our coffee from you, would that put your mind at rest? In other words, would you be happy to buy from us then?[13]

Buyer: I don't see why not. But I think you're going to have a tough job convincing me.

Salesperson: Well, let me deal with the issue head-on. You're worried about the risk; let's look at the risk.[14] In fact, let's look at the financial risk first. I think I told you last time that we do three starter packs – one at £500, one at £250 and one at £150. Do you remember that?

Buyer: Yes.

Salesperson: OK, let's take the cheapest pack for example, the one at £150. There's enough coffee bags in it to serve over 1800 coffees. Now let's suppose that you don't charge £1.80 per coffee – the price you were worried about a moment ago – let's assume instead that you only charge an

---

[11] You welcome the objection.
[12] You probe gently for clarification.
[13] You test the objection to see if it is genuine.
[14] You answer the objection by tackling it head-on.

average of £1.50. That would still give you sales of £2,700 from the one starter pack.

Buyer: If I sold all the coffee in it, yes.

Salesperson: Well, let's look at the risk involved. The pack costs £150, which means as soon as you've sold 100 coffees – or just over 5 per cent of your stock – then the whole lot's paid for. Even if you only sell 20 coffees a day for instance – and none of my present customers do less than 40 coffees a day – it'll only take you five days to eliminate the risk completely. Now, surely, that's not really a huge problem, is it?

Buyer: Maybe not when you put it like that, but I'm still not sure that my customers are the sort to adapt to this type of thing.

Salesperson: It's not just your customers, Mr Jones, it's all customers everywhere. No customer automatically adapts to new things without being given a bit of a nudge. We of all people know that; that's why we supply you with all the eye-catching menus and all the other signs I mentioned. It's this bright, interesting material that makes all the difference. It really does tempt people and, when people are tempted, they buy.[15]

Buyer: I can think of several customers of mine who wouldn't be in the least bit interested in buying coffee.

Salesperson: Of course you can. Not everyone is going to be tempted; but enough will be. Enough to show you a nice healthy profit. Remember what I told you last time about how nearly all the hotel managers I sell to come back to me within 14 days to reorder. I'm not saying that all your customers are going to start drinking Dutch or Viennese coffee, for instance, but a reasonable number will, and that's all you need.

Buyer: Hmmm.

Salesperson: There is one other point which is worth mentioning.[16] Although, as I said last time, we are the market leaders for this sort of luxury coffee and deal with hundreds of hotels up and down the country, there are still an awful

---

[15] A perfect example of how to empathize with your buyer's concerns and then use them to aid your presentation.

[16] You keep talking! The buyer is not yet convinced, so any pause or hesitation at this juncture would be fatal This is where your key information boxes come in handy.

lot of hotels who still serve nothing but the old standard instant coffee. This means that when a hotel does offer its customers a choice – when it does make a feature of its coffee – it stands out. All of a sudden, it has that extra something. And its customers are bound to appreciate it. I mean, it's a fairly competitive world isn't it; we can all do with that little 'edge', whatever sort of business we're in. Wouldn't you agree?

Buyers: I suppose so.

Salesperson: Well, that's the proposition, Mr Jones, it's got good potential for making quite sizeable profits – after all, sales of £2,700 from an outlay of £150 is pretty spectacular – and, at the same time, as I've just shown you, the risk is minimal. Your customers are bound to see the service you offer and enough of them are bound to be tempted. In any case, you only have to sell a tiny fraction of your stock and you're already making money. You really can't lose.[17] So why don't you let me put you down for one of our starter packs and we can get you taking money straightaway?

At this point the buyer will react in one of two ways. Either (1) he will accept what you say and give you the order, or (2) because he has already indicated that he is not going to make it easy for you to convince him, he will continue to resist. These reactions are dealt with in sequence. Once again, the alternative method of closing is used.

1.   Buyer gives way

Buyer: I must admit it doesn't sound too bad.

Salesperson: Well, it certainly makes good business sense, that's for sure. I think the only real question now is which starter pack you should take. I presume, from what you've said, that the luxury starter-pack, the £500 one, is just a bit out of your range?

Buyer: Yes. I don't think we could manage that one.

Salesperson: What about the mid-price one, the one at £250?

Buyer: No, I think I'm going to go for the smallest one – the one at £150.

Salesperson: That's fine. I'll get that off to you today.

You have closed the sale.

---

[17] Another example of an argument that you have thought out in advance.

2.   An example of the alternative close

Buyer: I don't know.

Salesperson: What have you got to lose, Mr Jones?

Buyer: I'm still not convinced the whole thing will work.

Salesperson: Why?

Buyer: I can't see my customers spending £1.50 on a coffee.

Salesperson: It's not just any old coffee, Mr Jones, it is real, fresh coffee. It's certainly a much higher quality coffee than your average instant brand.

Buyer: Oh, I realize that.

Salesperson: But your customers already pay nearly £1 for ordinary coffee. I mean, if they're capable of appreciating the difference between stewing beef and fillet steak, I assume they can do the same when it comes to coffee. All you've got to do it give them the choice and they'll show you, believe me.[18]

Buyer: Hmmm.

Salesperson: I'll tell you, I deal with hotel managers and hotel owners up and down the country every day and, believe me, after they've spent a couple of weeks selling our coffee they all invariably say the same thing: 'We never realized it would be so popular ... can we have some more?[18] I'm sure it will be the same for you, Mr Jones. So how about it? You've got nothing to lose. Which starter pack do you want to try – the big one, the medium one or the small one.[19]

Buyer: Well, definitely not the big one.

Salesperson: The medium one then.

Buyer: No, I think the small one.

Salesperson: OK, no problem, you can always come back for more when you need it. I'll get on to that right now.

You have closed the sale.

---

[18] You use your key information boxes and you keep talking.
[19] The alternative close in action! You avoid asking *whether* he will buy a starter pack – in case he says 'No'. Instead, you ask *which* starter pack he wants. You thus steer him into a corner from which it is difficult to escape.

Appendix

Example No 1: The complete script
NB: this is a verbal script. It needs to be 'spoken' rather than 'read'.

The canvassing call

Salesperson: Hello, Mr Smith. I don't think that we have spoken together before. My name is Sarah Brown. I work for Easiprint Limited. We supply a range of stationery items to several hundred companies throughout the London area: everything from typing and computer paper to adding machines and staplers. Not the most exciting stuff in the world, I'm afraid, but it keeps offices running nice and smoothly... [pause to allow the buyer to interject].

Buyer: [grunts]

Salesperson: The reason I'm ringing is really just to introduce myself. I don't want to go into chapter and verse about how good our stationery service is or why people buy from us, just at the moment – I think it's probably a bit soon for that. What I *would* like to do, if you can spare me a moment, is to ask you exactly what your company *does*. For example, I have you down as an electrical wholesaler. Is that correct?

Buyer: Yes.

Salesperson: And what sort of electrical products do you specialize in?

Buyer: All types: cookers, ovens, washing machines, tumble dryers, fridges, heaters, vacuum cleaners.

Salesperson: And whom do you sell to, in the main?

Buyer: Mostly shops but also to individuals at a public counter.

Salesperson:	How are you finding business overall?
Buyer:	Getting better.
Salesperson:	What about repairs? How are you involved in repairs?
Buyer:	Oh, we do quite a lot.
Salesperson:	Roughly how many office or administration staff do you have?
Buyer:	About ten.
Salesperson:	To what extent are you computerized?
Buyer:	All our stock and all accounts are fully computerized.
Salesperson:	And how do you get your stationery at the moment?
Buyer:	We just use one local distributor.
Salesperson:	How often do you usually order?
Buyer:	About once a fortnight.
Salesperson:	Finally, can I ask you what you look for in a stationery supplier?
Buyer:	Fast, reliable service.
Salesperson:	Listen, Mr Smith. Thanks very much indeed for your time and trouble. The information you've given me will be a great help. What I'll do now, is to send you our special information pack on the stationery service we provide, so you can see for yourself exactly what we offer. I'll leave it with you for a couple of days and give you a ring, say, Friday and we can then discuss the matter in a little more detail. How's that?
Buyer:	OK.
Salesperson:	When's the best time to get hold of you?
Buyer:	Oh, make it the morning.
Salesperson:	About 9.30?
Buyer:	Yes, that's fine.
Salesperson:	Right, I'll call you Friday at 9.30. Thanks very much, Mr Smith.

The presentation call

Salesperson:	Hello, Mr Smith. If you recall, we spoke together at the

	beginning of the week about the stationery service we provide for companies in the London area. It's Sarah Brown here, from Easiprint.
Buyer:	Oh, yes.
Salesperson:	Now, since we spoke, you should have received the special information pack I sent you, which explains all about us. Do you remember getting it?
Buyer:	Vaguely, yes.
Salesperson:	Good, I'll come to that in a moment. First, if possible, I'd like to go back over a couple of things you told me last time about how your company works and so on. For example, I think you said that both your stock and your accounts are fully computerized. Is that right?
Buyer:	Yes.
Salesperson:	And I presume, therefore, that most of your basic paperwork – delivery notes, invoices, statements and so on – is printed by the computer itself, none of it is preprinted?
Buyer:	That's right.
Salesperson:	You must be getting through a fair amount of computer paper then?
Buyer:	'Fraid so.
Salesperson:	What other stationery do you get through, in quantity?
Buyer:	Oh, envelopes, typing paper, few computer files, pens, that sort of thing.
Salesperson:	Typewriter ribbons?
Buyer:	Oh, yes.
Salesperson:	Can you think of anything else? I mean things that you order regularly.
Buyer:	Not really.
Salesperson:	OK, now you said last time that – at the moment – you buy all your stationery from one local supplier. Is that right?
Buyer:	Yes, we just use the one.
Salesperson:	What's his catalogue like; does he carry most of the stuff you need?

Buyer:	Yes, most of it.
Salesperson:	And anything he hasn't got, I presume, he can order for you?
Buyer:	Yes, that's right.
Salesperson:	OK, now what about ordering? I think you told me that you usually order fortnightly?
Buyer:	Usually, yes.
Salesperson:	And you can get away with that, I presume, because most of your business is fairly regular – you don't have any sudden mad rushes or anything like that?
Buyer:	Not usually, no.
Salesperson:	So you don't usually need your stationery delivered overnight?
Buyer.	No.
Salesperson:	But what you need, I presume, is a supplier who is *reliable* – in other words, someone who can guarantee to get you what you want and who can get it for you at a good price, would that be right?
Buyer:	I wouldn't disagree with that.
Salesperson:	So, if I can demonstrate a better service and lower prices than you are getting at the moment, then really you'd be a fool not to give us a try, wouldn't you?
Buyer:	Well, I might think about it.
Salesperson:	OK. Well let me deal with the service side of things first. To begin with, because we're larger and probably deal with a lot more customers than your local supplier, we've got the resources to make it easy for you to deal with us. For example, you don't have to ring us, we ring you. In fact, we'll arrange to ring you once a week – or more often if you prefer that – at whatever time suits you. As well as that, the person who rings you will know exactly what you are talking about. So if you're worried about product compatibility, for instance, they'll tell you what's compatible and what isn't. If you've heard about a new product, for example, the chances are first, that they'll know about it, and second that we'll be getting it in stock. What I'm really saying is that we want to make life as easy for you as we can.

Buyer: What about when you run out of stock?

Salesperson: I'll come to that in just a moment. OK, we ring you once a week to take your order. It'll then be packed the same day and delivered by special courier 48 hours later. Now, if by chance you forget to put something urgent on your order, or you suddenly find you're going to run out of something, don't worry. You can always get through to us. We've got over 30 telephone lines, and we have an emergency overnight courier service to make sure that anything you order (up to 4 pm) will be delivered to you before lunchtime the following day. So basically, whatever your particular need is, we can fix it. Now you asked about out of stock problems?

Buyer: That's right. How often do you run out of stock?

Salesperson: You mean how often are we out of stock of things like computer paper, typing paper, envelopes, typewriter ribbons, pens, that sort of thing? The things you need all the time?

Buyer: Yes.

Salesperson: Never.

Buyer: I don't believe it.

Salesperson: Well, check what we say in the brochure. You see all the items I mentioned are down in our catalogue as Grade A items. And all Grade A items are *always* in stock. That's why so many companies use us. And there's no magic to it, we just carry huge stocks of all the most common items. That's why we never run out.

Buyer: What about less common items?

Salesperson: Less common items are what we call Grade B stuff. They include things like specialized rubber stamps, certain types of expandable files, electronic adding machines, and so on. Now, even as far as this stuff is concerned, we're rarely, if ever, out of stock. And even if we are, we guarantee to be in stock within three days, so in practice it's not a problem. I mean, to give you a concrete example, yesterday we sent out over 85 orders with about 1,000 items in them: and out of all of that, only one item was marked out of stock, and that was one of our 'top of the range' adding machines. Now that's not bad, is it?

Buyer: No, not bad.

Salesperson: Right, so the service *works*. It's reliable, it's easy and it doesn't break down because of out-of-stock problems. You won't, for example, find that we have to order items for you, to be delivered as and when we get round to it and you won't have any more worries about not being able to send out invoices because your printer's run out of paper. Now I call that a first-class service. How about you?

Buyer: It's not bad. What about the money side of things?

Salesperson: That's the second bit of good news. Because we buy in such large quantities, we get very good prices, which in turn we pass on to you. For instance, what do you normally pay for an 'X' typewriter ribbon, just taking it as an example? I'd say probably about £4, excluding VAT?

Buyer: About that.

Salesperson: Well, for the 'X' ribbon we charge £3.75, excluding VAT, and we also stock the 'Y' ribbon – which is every bit as good as the 'X', in practice – and that only costs £3.45. Now these are only examples, I could quote you dozens of others and every one of them would be a step lower than the prices you're paying at the moment. I mean, I'll be frank with you: it would be worth your while switching to us for the better service *alone*, never mind the lower prices. But when you can also save a fair amount of money on top of that, well, really, you'd be daft not to give us a try, wouldn't you?

Buyer: It's worth thinking about anyway.

Salesperson: OK. Well, before we got any further, can you think of anything I haven't covered? Is there anything else about the service which you want to know, which I haven't mentioned?

Buyer: What about credit terms? I assume you give 30 days' credit as usual?

Salesperson: Yes, that's all standard.

Buyer: In that case, I think you've covered just about everything.

Salesperson: OK, so how about putting together a first order for us? That way we can actually show you how good we are. Can you get one prepared by Monday, for example?

Buyer:	Hmmm. I'm not sure. I'll have to think about it first.
Salesperson:	Sure, have a think about it. While I'm on the phone, though, can I ask you how you feel about what I've told you? Are you satisfied with everything or is there something you're not quite sure about?
Buyer:	No, it all sounds pretty reasonable. I just need the weekend to think about it, that's all.
Salesperson:	No problem. How about if I call you, say, first thing on Tuesday? We can go over anything I haven't mentioned then.
Buyer:	Yes, that's fine.
Salesperson:	OK, now finally, before I go, what about the big match on Saturday, the Rugby International? Who do you fancy, England or Wales?
Buyer:	Actually I can't stand rugby. Football is more my game.
Salesperson:	Oh, which team do you follow?
Buyer:	York City.
Salesperson:	York City? Who are they? Are they some sort of amateur team?
Buyer:	Cheeky beggar. They're top of the Fourth Division at the moment.

The salesperson should now bring the conversation to a close by reminding the buyer to expect a call from him first thing on Tuesday.

The closing call

Salesperson:	Hello, Mr Smith. I hope you had a good weekend. It's Sarah Brown here from Easiprint, the stationers. If you remember, we spoke at the end of last week.
Buyer:	Oh, yes.
Salesperson:	I said I'd call you this morning in order to go over anything I didn't mention last time and take your first order. How are things looking?
Buyer:	Actually I haven't really had a chance to decide what I'm going to do yet. Perhaps you could leave it with me until next week sometime.
Salesperson:	I could do, but wouldn't the best thing be to actually show you our service in *practice*?

Buyer:	How do you mean?
Salesperson:	Well, I think I told you all about our service last time. I explained how we guarantee always to be in stock of the items you need. I also went over our prices with you, which, from memory, were quite a bit lower than the ones you are paying at the moment. So you've *got* all the information: the only thing that remains now is for us to demonstrate our service in practice. So why not draw up a small order for us and put us to the test? I mean, as they say, actions speak louder than words.
Buyer:	I'm not sure.
Salesperson:	Well, let's start with a couple of things you always need. Say, typewriter ribbons and computer paper. You said last time that you pay roughly £4 a ribbon. How much do you pay for your computer paper – about £3.50 a box?
Buyer:	Er … no. About £3.20.
Salesperson:	And would I be right in assuming that you get through about ten ribbons and about 50 boxes of paper a fortnight?
Buyer:	About that.
Salesperson:	Right, I'm just doing some calculations at this end, because I want you to see the difference in *practice* between using us and using anyone else. If you buy ten 'X' ribbons – the sort you normally use – and 50 boxes of standard-width computer paper from your normal supplier, then, according to the figures you've given me, you pay £40 for your ribbons and £160 for your paper, which makes a total of £200. However, if you give me an order for exactly the same items, your company will only pay a total of £180 – that's a saving of 10 per cent or £20 on just one order. Enough to buy another seven boxes of computer paper. Now surely, Mr Smith, when your company can save that much money on just one order, isn't it worth giving us a try?

At this point, the buyer will probably react in one of two ways. Either (1) he will begin to appreciate the logic of what you are saying and grudgingly recognize that his interests are best served by giving you a trial order or (2) he will stand his ground and continue to hold out. These reactions are dealt with in sequence. In both cases the salesperson employs the *alternative* method of closing the sale.

(1) The buyer gives way

Buyer: I see what you mean.

Salesperson: Well, let me make a suggestion. Why don't we both put the whole thing to the test? Either let me put together an order for you – say just the ten ribbons and the 50 boxes of paper we talked about a moment ago – or, alternatively, you put one together yourself and I'll call you back in half an hour to take the details. Tell me which option you prefer, and we can then get on with things and let our service speak for itself.

Buyer: Hmmm. I think it's probably better if I do the order. There may be one or two other things we need.

Salesperson: Fine. How about if I call you in about half an hour?

Buyer: OK. I should have it ready for you by then.

You have closed the sale.

(2) The buyer stands his ground and objects

Buyer: I'm still not sure. Price isn't everything.

Salesperson: I agree, price by itself may not be important at all. In fact, in this case, I get the feeling that you're more concerned about the actual service we offer, rather than our prices. Am I right?

Buyer: Yes.

Salesperson: Does this mean, though, that if I reassure you that our service can genuinely give you everything you could reasonably expect from a supplier, then you'll be happy to deal with us? That the service plus the low prices will put your mind at rest?

Buyer: I suppose so, yes.

Salesperson: OK, well let's focus for a moment on what can go wrong with the service and I'll see if I can reassure you about a few things. Are you worried about us being out of stock, for example?

Buyer: Yes, that is a worry.

Salesperson: Well, you can now stop worrying. I don't know what your present supplier is like, but at Easiprint we just don't have that problem. As I explained last time, we operate a very strict system of stock control and we genuinely have huge stocks of all the basic stationery items. Now in practice, 90 per cent of all your orders will be for this sort of basic stationery – or what we call Grade A items – and we guarantee *never* to be out of stock of any of it. I mean, you can't ask more than that, can you?

Buyer: Not really, I suppose.

Salesperson: As far as the less common items are concerned, as I've said, we hardly ever run out of stock of these items either, and, if we do, we guarantee to have them back in stock within three working days. Now I assume that puts your mind at rest regarding stock problems?

Buyer: Hmmm . . . I think so.

Salesperson: What about delivery, is that a worry too?

Buyer: Well, since you're not local, yes it is.

Salesperson: OK, once again you can relax because there is nothing to worry about. We use a first-class courier service and we guarantee delivery anywhere south of Birmingham within 48 hours. Plus, if its urgent, we can deliver anything you order before 4 pm by lunchtime the following day.

Buyer: And how much does this delivery cost?

Salesperson: For all orders of £20 or more our standard delivery is completely free.

Buyer: Hmmm.

Salesperson: Now, tell me what else you're not absolutely sure about.

Buyer: What if something is damaged or faulty?

Salesperson: No problem. Just send it back. You get a credit straight away.

Buyer [says nothing]

Salesperson: Anything else?

Buyer: Not that I can think of.

Salesperson: Right. I've shown you how using us will save you money. I trust that now I have also put your mind at rest about our service and how it functions in practice. So I've done *my* bit. Now all *you* have to do is to give me a trial order and put us to the test. How about it?

Buyer: [pausing for a moment] Well, I suppose it all sounds reasonable.

Salesperson: OK, well what's the best thing to do? Do you want *me* to put together an order for *you* – say the ten ribbons and the 50 boxes of computer paper we talked about earlier – or would you prefer to do one yourself and have me call back in half an hour to take the details?

Buyer: I suppose you might as well do the order. Make it for five ribbons, though, and 30 boxes of paper and we'll see about anything else afterwards.

Salesperson: That's fine, Mr Smith. I'll do the order now myself and you'll have it on Thursday.

The sale is closed.

Further Reading from Kogan Page

Auer, J T: *Inspired Selling: A Book of Ideas, Opportunities and Renewal*
Denny, Richard: *Selling to Win: Tested Techniques for Closing the Sale*
Golis, Christopher C: *Empathy Selling: The Powerful New Technique for the 1990s*
Ley D Forbes: *The Best Seller*
Schiffman, Stephan: *Cold Calling Techniques*
       The 25 Most Common Sales Mistakes ... and How to Avoid Them
Thomson, Peter: *Sell Your Way to the Top*
Tirbutt, Edmund: *How to Increase Sales Without Leaving Your Desk*
Vicar, Robert: *First Division Selling*
      Prospecting for Customers
Weymes, Pat: *How to Perfect Your Selling Skills*

A full list is available from the publisher.